The Mission Table

The Mission Table

Renewing Congregation and Community

✖ ✖ ✖

Stephen P. Bouman

AUGSBURG FORTRESS

Minneapolis

THE MISSION TABLE
Renewing Congregation and Community

Book of Faith is an initiative of the

 Evangelical Lutheran Church in America
God's work. Our hands.

For information on the Book of Faith initiative and Book of Faith resources, go to www .bookoffaith.org.

ISBN 978-1-4514-7812-9

Cover design: Laurie Ingram
Interior design and typesetting: PerfecType, Nashville, TN

The paper used in this publication meets the minimum requirements of American National Standard for Information Sciences—Permanence of Paper for Printed Library Materials, ANSI Z329.48-1984.

Manufactured in the U.S.A.

18 17 16 15 14 13   2 3 4 5 6 7 8 9 10

Contents

worship: joy; strength for service;
   healing; learning thru Word, pictures,
   symbols; forgiveness; ↑ sense of
   family/community; truth

Ball&chain vs. helium baloon.
Turn our "swords to plowshares"
           "mourning to dancing"

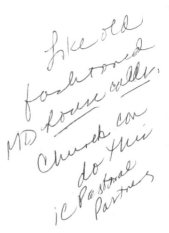

Foreword

What are your expectations of the Holy Spirit? Before you begin to read *The Mission Table*, take time to ponder that question and write down your responses.

When you read the scriptures, what are your expectations of the Holy Spirit? What do you expect the Holy Spirit will accomplish when you gather for worship? If I asked you to describe what the Holy Spirit is up to in and through your congregation, to what would you give witness? What are the hopes and the hurts, the fears and the faith of those who live in the community around your congregation? How would they describe the good life? Who are the neglected, the isolated who assume no one knows their names and who have no table to which they are welcomed?

In *The Mission Table*, my colleague Pastor Stephen Bouman invites us—challenges us—to be a church with high expectations of the Holy Spirit. He assumes the Holy Spirit is not done with us yet. Through the good news of Jesus Christ, the Holy Spirit is at work making us new creations in Christ, reconciling the alienated, forgiving us and setting us free for lives of witness and service. The Holy Spirit is at work tearing down the walls that divide us and turning those walls into tables of reconciliation and conversation. Christ welcomes all to the table of his presence.

No congregation is absent the power and presence of the Holy Spirit. Not one of us lacks gifts of the Spirit. Christ risen from the dead means there are no godforsaken places or God-forgotten people. Yet we sometimes forget Jesus promised that we will receive power when the Holy Spirit comes on us. That is especially true when we describe the church on the basis of what we lack and have lost and nostalgically long for days gone by.

We have all that we need: God's promise. So we begin by listening. We listen to God's promises spoken to God's people throughout the scriptures. We listen to one another as we discern the gifts the Spirit has given for the sake of the gospel and the common good. We listen to the life stories of those who live in the communities around us. In those three great listenings, we believe the Holy Spirit is at work renewing us, restoring us, and sending us to be about God's work for the life of the world. We go because we believe our neighbors deserve to hear the good news of God's love for them. We go anointed with the power of the Spirit.

And we do not go alone. I encourage you to study *The Mission Table* with members of other congregations in your community. Invite those who have no community of faith to listen with you. Enter your study of this book with high expectations of the Holy Spirit.

But beware! Because when the Holy Spirit shows up, lives are changed— the dead are raised, demons are cast out, sins are forgiven, despair gives way to hope, unbelief turns to faith, the alienated are reconciled, those in poverty hear good news, people sell their possessions and give to the poor, and all are welcome at the table. Pentecost was not a onetime event. Jesus promised to send the Holy Spirit, the Advocate, who reminds us when we forget God's faithfulness to God's promise and empowers us to do even greater deeds than Jesus did (John 14).

What a cause for high expectations of the Holy Spirit!

Day of Pentecost 2013
Mark S. Hanson, Presiding Bishop
Evangelical Lutheran Church in America

Mission and the Mainline

From one ancestor [God] made all nations to inhabit the whole earth, and he allotted the times of their existence and the boundaries of the places where they would live, so that they would search for God and perhaps grope for him and find him. Tho indeed he is not far from us.

—Acts 17:26-27

Stoics
Epicureans
altar to "an unknown god" in Athens
St Paul
Athens

Over the past few years, we have become accustomed to headlines in the press declaring the demise of mainline Protestant Christianity—for example, a January 2013 cover story in *The Lutheran* titled "The Shrinking Church" and a 2012 editorial in the *New York Times* titled "The Decline of the Mainline." Some prognosticators are moving beyond "shrinking" and "declining" to pronounce "death" for Lutheran, Episcopal, Presbyterian, United Church of Christ, Methodist, and other mainline Protestant denominations. Although I believe the death knell is premature, there is no question that our churches are declining, that the public cultural context in which the church lives is in the midst of massive change, that an emerging generation is largely absent from church, and that these things have been going on for a long time. Among the more than ten thousand congregations

1

of the Evangelical Lutheran Church in America (ELCA), some are shrinking in size, some are dying, some are thriving, and many are labeled "at risk" by various measurements, but they are not going away anytime soon.

Engaging the Conversation

This book on the mission of the church is written with full acknowledgment of the deteriorating and shrinking forms of life and mission for mainline congregations and institutions, but also with the conviction that these communities of Jesus are still, or can be again, vital to God's mission in the world. I believe our decline is tinged with hope, and we in the ELCA want to join and move forward a conversation about mission that is energizing the Lutheran church and our mainline partners.

Mainline churches are working hard to address the present disconnect between the church and the world and to live into a new future. Many so-called emerging faith communities and mission probes are changing the church's "front door"—referring to where and how new people enter a congregation—from worship style to service to struggle for the souls of our communities. Many of these "emerging" mission communities are with young adults.

As we think about today's context for mission, consider the situation of the apostle Paul on Mars Hill (Acts 17). Paul noticed the many diverse ways that faith and spiritual seeking flowered in Athens. He took these spiritual journeys seriously and sought to understand and respect them. He practiced the great foundational mission act of *listening* by hearing the stories of his neighbors and noticing their spiritual journeys. From the heart of what he heard, he shared his own story: the death and resurrection of Jesus for the life of the world. He joined their spiritual conversation, saying, "What . . . you worship as unknown, this I proclaim to you" (v. 23).

Engaging Leaders

The conversation about mission must include laypeople, pastors, seminarians, and emerging congregational leaders. Leaders for mission today must work differently than we have in the past. Over thirty years ago, I graduated from seminary with a set of skills that helped me teach and interpret scripture, and enabled me to manage the congregational structures in place when I arrived at my first pastorate. I was also trained in providing pastoral care for and with the faithful. Evangelism was the stilted activity of one of many ongoing committees.

Today leadership that manages existing congregational structures, takes care of the members, and does strategic planning as if knowing what the future holds will no longer suffice for the mission of the church and our congregations. We cannot assume that our culture, or even members of our congregations, can tell the old, old story of the biblical drama or that they know the forms, songs, and prayers of the liturgy.

Leaders today must be prepared to come alongside a congregation and its individual members and be willing to reroot the life of that congregation in the life of its community. Leaders today must join members and neighbors in their spiritual journeys, hearing their disappointments, questions, and hopes. They must agitate for mission imagination and courage and be willing to see old things die and risk new things being born. Their focus must be on helping people embrace their baptismal vocation.

Talking about Mission

Mission is one of those words used often for many different reasons. Mission statements drive the work of businesses, nonprofits, the local bowling league, and even our churches. When I speak about the *mission of the church* in these pages, I mean *God's reconciling and restoring action in the world*. Scholars of mission have called this the *missio Dei* (mission of God). Broadly this movement of God in the world draws all creation to the fullness that God intends. We sometimes call this the reign of God or kingdom of God. In faith we believe this is happening all around us all the time, and part of our faith journey is to look for ways in which we can participate. God is present in the world.

Martin Luther's comment on the second petition of the Lord's Prayer—"Your kingdom come"—echoes this belief: "God's kingdom comes on its own without our prayer, but we ask in this prayer that it may also come to us."[1]

For Christians, our baptism in the life, death, and resurrection of Jesus pulls us all toward this mission in the name of Jesus. Lutherans and other Protestants call this Christian vocation "the priesthood of all believers." In our baptism into the death and resurrection of Jesus Christ, we become a part of the body of Christ in the world. Jesus' mission of healing, reconciling, and restoring identity becomes our own.

Lutherans have a distinct contribution to make to a conversation about mission. Our central tenets of sacramental vitality, grace, the vocation of the priesthood of all believers, and a "two-handed" God at work in the world while leading this present time toward eternity undergird the discussion. This image of God reflects Martin Luther's "two kingdoms" theology, which speaks of a God active both in the everyday events of human history and in the ultimate salvation of all creation.

Table is a central image for this book. Table is about relationships and community. The tables of our lives center our trust in a God who is perfect relationship. The God we call the Holy Trinity and in whom we have been baptized is perfect love and community. The fullness of this God is pleased to dwell in this world in the life, death, and resurrection of Jesus.

What shapes the tables of our communities of Jesus, each baptized disciple, and his or her mission in the world is the biblical drama of the story of Israel; the paschal mystery of the life, mission, death, and resurrection of Jesus; and the New Testament church that emerged from these narratives.

Our tables are expressions, in the name of Jesus, of God's love and community:

- The perfect table of creation, where all creation was in harmony with the Creator.
- The broken table and the sorrow and death of this world, which has lost its perfect community and mutual relationship with the Creator.
- The kitchen table where we heard stories of our biblical and familial ancestors, where our faith, culture, and values were formed.
- The altar table of our congregations, which unites the kitchen tables of our parishes.

- New tables that we form with our neighbors: tables of renewal, reconciled relationships, and restored vision for the life of the world God loves.

Mission tables take shape when kitchen and altar tables merge with new and renewed tables in the community locally and globally—where new relationships of mutuality and reconciliation are formed for the life of the world. I refer to this process as "rerooting in the community." Here we practice the *three great listenings*: listening to God, listening to one another in the church, and listening to our neighbors in the community. The ELCA's global mission is driven by such listening in a movement called *accompaniment*, a term I will also use in this discussion.

I will use the word *Eucharist* to describe the sacrament of Holy Communion, the Lord's Supper. *Eucharist* is a rich table word that means "thanksgiving" in Greek. It reminds us that Jesus at the table with his disciples said a table prayer like many of us have experienced. He took bread, then wine, and each time gave thanks for it, reminding us of our good Creator.

Using This Book

This book is meant to be used in congregations by lay leaders, pastors, and rostered leaders, and also by seminarians, participants in lay schools and lifelong learning programs, mission developers, synod leaders and staff, and other denominational leaders.

Each of the chapters is infused with scripture and the questions and activities lend themselves to group study, reflection, and action. In addition, the Model for Congregation Listening Tables (pages 99-101) can help congregations and other groups in their initial vision and plans for setting listening tables.

Group discussion of the seven chapters and introduction can be configured in a number of ways. One approach that congregations might consider is a three-module format offered over the course of a year:

Module A: Tables (introduction, chapters 1–3)
    Session 1: Mission and the Mainline (introduction)
    Session 2: The Table of Creation (chapter 1)

A congregation could work through these modules on two tracks: the first could be for the congregation council alone, and then the council could invite leaders of other teams in the congregation to participate. For example, a congregation council could begin with Module A following the annual congregational meeting, and after three to four months move to Module B. As this central leadership team engages in conversation about biblical marks of a missional congregation (Module B), other leaders could begin with Module A. Then, after three to four months, the central leadership team could move on to Module C and the leaders of other congregational teams could begin Module B, with all leaders having completed the process in approximately sixteen months. In addition, all congregational members could be engaged in the process through sermons and Bible studies based on the central Bible passages woven through the book. This is just one model. Many other approaches are possible, and you will know best what will work in your setting.

So That All Would Search for God (Acts 17:27)

Congregations on the Mars Hill of today's diverse, global society have a role to play, much like that of the apostle Paul's: to listen, to engage, to fashion new tables while communally groping for God in the world, to live as signs of the God who made the world and who will make all things new.

CHAPTER 1

The Table of Creation

---

*Then I saw a new heaven and a new earth. . . . And I saw the holy city, the
new Jerusalem, coming down out of heaven from God. . . . And I heard a
loud voice from the throne saying,*

> *"See, the home of God is among mortals.*
> *[God] will dwell with them;*
> *they will be [God's] peoples,*
> *and God . . . will be with them;*
> *[God] will wipe every tear from their eyes.*
> *Death will be no more;*
> *mourning and crying and pain will be no more,*
> *for the first things will have passed away."*

. . . "See, I am making all things new."

—Revelation 21:1-5

[handwritten note: "God's hands are ours"]

[handwritten note: ELCA theme for 25th anniversary]

Chang Lee survived two brutal wars in his home country, Korea. He
lived through Japanese bombs, Chinese howitzers, North Korean
mine fields, and American carbines. But he did not survive an encounter
with a mugger in the hallway of his apartment in Queens, New York. He
was brutally stabbed and ended his earthly journey at the age of eighty.

He and his family were members of Atonement Lutheran, the congregation I served in Queens. His son was one of the leaders of the large Korean group that was part of our multicultural congregation. At the crowded funeral, lessons and prayers were offered in English and Korean. The casket was set up like a Shinto shrine, with pictures of the deceased, flowers, and two posters in Korean ideograms. One poster gave biographical details, the other was the Twenty-Third Psalm. Placed in Chang Lee's dead hands was his tattered Korean New Testament, giving mute testimony to the faith that was his companion on his lifelong journey from East to West, from life to death . . . to life.

Chang Lee died a Christian. He died a Korean. The service was marked by Oriental politeness, form, respect, ancestral devotion. The liturgy provided an occasion for those gathered to express great emotion, to cry, to lift up the cross, to sing with verve "How Great Thou Art" and "Rock of Ages," to nod and mutter "amen" and even to smile at me as I spoke of the love of Christ that enfolds all creation and holds it before the Creator.

A motorcade of forty cars wended its way down the crowded Long Island expressway to the cemetery. After the graveside committal, each of the family members bowed low before the casket in respect and deference to another ancestor in the communion of saints. Then something remarkable happened, something I had never seen before. The entire funeral party began walking from the grave but not to their cars. They filed over to a nearby grove of trees, spread out blankets and food and drink, and had a picnic. One of the family members came over to me and smiled, handing me a sandwich and a soft drink. "Eat and drink, Pastor. Enjoy! Life goes on!" And so it did, as we ate and drank among the tombstones of the Pine Lawn Cemetery, celebrating life and hope in a place of the dead.

In the graveyard, Mr. Lee's family set a table.

Communing with God

The simple act of eating and drinking in the graveyard with the Lee family was sacramental; it was communion with the God of creation.

In the beginning, God set a table: all creation is a table of nurturing relationships created by the perfect community of the Trinity, God the Creator, Savior, and Sustainer. God's dream is oneness, mutuality, and the goodness of all creation. Human beings were created to serve at the table of creation, to participate in its unfolding in partnership with the triune Creator.

Each animal, plant, and seed was shot through with God's presence. The life between the man and the woman, the end of loneliness, the relationships between humans were also gifts of God and communion with the Creator. Life itself was sacramental, with every moment, every morsel of food, every surprise of beauty leading directly to the Creator, the giver of all good gifts.

In the beginning, Adam was made to be a steward priest, called to "bless" all creation by acknowledging the Creator, by partaking of creation as life from God. And the table of creation, this sweet world, was eucharist, with human beings as the ones who received it all as life from God. Adam offered it all back to God in the act of "naming" and having *dominion* over creation—that is, taking responsibility for it in obedience to the Creator. To bless, to name, to take responsibility, to eat and drink and partake with reverence and thanksgiving—that was the eucharistic life of humanity in the midst of God's creation.

After the fall, the perfect table of creation was broken. Adam and Eve left this perfection and went out into the world as mortal beings but bearing signs of the promised reconciliation of all creation and a memory of the first table.

A Broken Table

Today our immediate global connections via the Internet mean that a person can tell a joke in Copenhagen, and because of it, someone gets killed in Karachi. We are virtually connected throughout the world, yet some are suggesting that we are lonelier and more afraid than ever before. We create and curate images of ourselves on social media and launch them into play with a world of virtual creations. In the public arena, we feel like objects,

Cross in the Narthex hungry.
'outsiders' late, unworthy.

not subjects of our histories. Recent US elections and the attendant political gridlock in Congress are another reminder of how helpless and out of control we feel regarding decisions that affect the life of our world. We were created for solidarity, the collective power for dominion (responsibility in obedience to God) in creation. But that table has been broken.

The table is broken by racial, gender, class, and economic inequity. The table is broken by persistent violence in our homes and communities, a flawed immigration system, and the stubborn persistence of poverty. There is an enormous sense of dislocation in our society and in our churches. Things are changing so fast that congregations don't know what to do except what they have always done. In the broken connection between our altar tables and the table of creation, we are losing rootedness in our communities. *Made New*

In the garden, God called Adam and Eve to participate in ordering and nourishing the life of the world. But we retreat from participation in decisions that shape our world into the defended spaces of polar extremes, of "red state" and "blue state" divisions, creating solidarity and connections only with "people like us." Too often we make of our great public table in the midst of creation a private table haven from the world. We get lost in narrow church issues and fights as we retreat from collective action and responsibility, from the God-given mandate to participate in the life of the world as worship of the Creator.

Too often the sacramental life of the church replicates the broken table. A single-minded focus to set the table for those who are poor and the strangers among us and those without the gospel becomes diffused in issues of congregational survival. Prayer life becomes rote, communal study of scripture happens infrequently, evangelism is a committee not the commitment of every disciple. We go through the motions not expecting much. We tolerate losing our children and grandchildren and their generations from the table a chair at a time. The old, old story just becomes old and infrequently told. We lose our curiosity and our embrace of our communities. The table is ours, not the world's. *Lord's Table*

In the beginning, at the table of creation, all of life was sacramental, an ongoing eucharist. Now the grace of God is dispensed in moments, like medicine, to make the person "better"—in a thimbleful of water, a dash of oil, "christening" but not "drowning" at the font. Even Sunday eating and drinking is often a private table, a picnic ignoring the tombstones, a catered escape from the world.

And yet perhaps the most radical and holy thing anyone can do is to repair a table, set a table, reconnect table to table.

Creation in the Eucharist, the Eucharist in Creation

Eating and drinking are primal communion with God. The hunger of Adam and Eve, which is also our own, is a hunger for God. God satisfies that hunger with all of creation.

In the Eucharist, all creation joins Christ in his journey to the Father. Jesus, our Brother and ancestor, is the Christ who in his ascension heads up all creation. He is the *fullness* of all things.

At the Eucharist, the presider, in the ministry of Christ, stands in the midst of creation and offers it to the Creator as eucharistic praise. The world is again in communion with God. Eating and drinking are again holy, for the object is no longer the food but the presence of God.

In the Eucharist, our faith becomes concrete, carnal, when in the eating and drinking we participate in the death and resurrection of the firstborn of all creation, Jesus the Christ, who at the cross promised, "I, when I am lifted up . . . will draw all people to myself" (John 12:32).

When we celebrate the Lord's Supper, this liturgy takes place in the midst of God's created world. And God's created world comes to the table.

The world is present at the Eucharist

- in the gifts of bread and wine.
- in the history of the lives of those who gather.
- as fruits of our labors, symbolized by our offering of money.

In villages in Nicaragua and Tanzania, the community brings to the altar their hoes, plows, fishing nets, and other implements of livelihood, as well as goats, eggs, bananas, and rice. They place them on the table, thus placing themselves on the table. All have gifts; all creation is a gift.

The world is present at the Eucharist

- in the intercessions of God's people, their yearning for peace, their anguish at the pain of life.
- as time: as God's people get out of bed, leave their kitchen tables, and come to the altar, they offer their "time," a slice of their history.
- in the diversity of the people.

Church can be, or sometimes is, one of the few places in our society where gifts can be given across generations and ethnicities. One of the joys of my thirty-five years of ministry among the 16 million people of the New York metropolitan area is that in the incredible ethnic diversity of New York's neighborhoods, the churches are literally in the midst of all the peoples of the world. The most recent US census has disclosed that global presence everywhere in America. Even in the most racially and ethnically homogeneous of parishes, a diversity of age, class, gender, values, aspirations, politics, and economics exists. As our population is aging, our communities are experiencing multiple generations together.

People bring their world to the altar in the celebration of the Eucharist, expecting in this eating and drinking a solidarity that includes them, is relevant to them, and enfolds their hopes, fears, suffering, and dreams. They long to place their stories on the table.

The Sunday after Chang Lee's funeral, the family was present at the Eucharist. The world was present with them, a world of tombstones and grief, dread and hope, joy and faith, and ancestors who are among "angels and archangels and all the company of heaven."

A Public Table

Imagine that you are celebrating this sacrament not behind the closed doors of the church but in the midst of Main Street and all the hustle and bustle of human life. At St. Peter's Lutheran Church in Manhattan, the sanctuary is located in a high-rise building with thousands of workers, at a busy subway stop from which thousands of commuters ascend directly toward the church. Windows of the sanctuary open up to the busy sidewalk, where those worshiping see the ebb and flow of pedestrians walking by or stopping to look into the windows at those around the table.

Imagining the table in the center of town or out on the highway is a reminder that this table exists to open us up to God's mission for the life of the world. Yes, the world is present at the Eucharist, and the way is open for the transformation of the world through the death and resurrection of Jesus. In our solidarity with Christ and one another, the renewed unity of all humanity begins to emerge. At this table, we are called to serve in solidarity with the world, a service that is one of reconciliation and kinship in suffering and hope with all people.

To celebrate the Eucharist in the midst of the world is to expose the false divisions of life. There is no sacred as opposed to secular. The Eucharist cannot be trivialized to "cultic rite," "right religion," or "spiritual exercise," or even a "faith practice," as if there were some domain in which Christ is not present.

To place the Eucharist in the midst of the world is not to baptize life with extraneous doses of God. It rather recognizes the presence of the incarnate Lord in everything. The earthly vessels of water, bread, and wine root the grace of God in the things of this world. We cannot spiritualize away the concrete context of God's love for the world any more than we can spiritualize out of existence a casket lowered into the hard earth or a sandwich eaten among the marble slabs of a cemetery. Altar and creation are one table in Christ.

God's people are called to sacramental living in the world. Our mission is to live eucharistically, as signs of the presence of God in everything. We who have been filled with the presence of Christ in the eating and drinking at the altar also see the presence of Christ in a picnic in the cemetery. Leaving the altar table filled with Christ's graceful presence, we hit the street and begin to notice the graceful presence of God in the world around us. We have been fed to point to that presence and join it. The church in the world understands that the restoring, reconciling, recreating reign of God is breaking into all the dark, anonymous corners of creation.

In the beginning, God set a table. Mission begins here.

Read and Reflect, Discuss and Reflect

1. Reread Revelation 21:1-5, which begins this chapter. What does it say to you, at this time and place, about God, the church, and the wider world?

2. When or where have you experienced solidarity with or the unity of God's creation?

3. How does your congregation reflect the diversity and unity of God's creation?

Grand Canyon – Psalm quotation 2ft x 2ft bronze plaque.

CHAPTER 2

From the Kitchen Table to the Altar Table

And Mary said,
"My soul magnifies the Lord,
    and my spirit rejoices in God my Savior,
for he has looked with favor on the lowliness of his servant.
    Surely, from now on all generations will call me blessed;
for the Mighty One has done great things for me,
    and holy is his name.
His mercy is for those who fear him
    from generation to generation.
He has shown strength with his arm;
    he has scattered the proud in the thoughts of their hearts.
He has brought down the powerful from their thrones,
    and lifted up the lowly;
he has filled the hungry with good things,
    and sent the rich away empty.
He has helped his servant Israel,
    in remembrance of his mercy,
according to the promise he made to our ancestors,
    to Abraham and to his descendants forever."

—Luke 1:46-55

For many of us, our faith is a gift given across the generations, a legacy of grandparents, aunts, uncles, parents, friends, pastors, and Sunday school teachers. For all of us, our faith has been formed and shaped in a community of believers who act as sign bearers and tell the story of God's vision for reconciliation, forgiveness, restoration, and grace.

When I walk the halls cradling my granddaughter, Sophia Grace, in my arms, rocking her gently as I try to put her to sleep, I sing love songs to her. They are the songs I sang to my children, because they are the songs my grandmother and my parents sang to me when they put me to bed, told me stories, and heard my prayers. "Now rest beneath night's shadow," I sing. "I am Jesus' little lamb, ever glad at heart I am . . ." "Jesus, Savior, wash away . . ." As I look into the drowsy eyes of Sophia Grace watching me sing, the idea of a legacy, of bequeathing something, seems like a life worth living.

As my cousin Walter Bouman was nearing death, he preached for the last time at Trinity Seminary in Columbus, Ohio, where he had taught for many years. He turned to the songs of his own mother and grandmother. In the sermon, he said, "When I first returned home from the hospital, I prayed each night that God would not let me wake up in this world. But then Anna Madsen (a former student assistant) sent me an email saying, 'Don't you dare die until I get to Columbus.' When Anna talks, even God listens. So I stopped praying that prayer. Instead, I have turned to a prayer sung to me as a child in German: 'Breit aus die Fluegel beide, o Jesu meine Freude, and nimm dein Kuechlein ein . . . Spread out both of your wings, O Jesus my Joy, and gather in your little chick.'"

And I sing to Sophia Grace the English translation of that same song sung to me as a child, a love song that goes like this:

> Lord Jesus, since you love me,
> now spread your wings above me
> and shield me from alarm.
> Though evil would assail me,
> your mercy will not fail me.
> I rest in your protecting arm.[2]

The opening chapters of Luke's gospel include a number of love songs, hymns of praise still known by their Latin names—Mary's Magnificat,

Zechariah's Benedictus, the angels' Gloria, and Simeon's Nunc dimittis—that reveal how the faith taught by our ancestors takes root in daily life.

To keep the love song going is at the heart of the church's mission.

The Kitchen Table

Do you remember your kitchen table? What was on it? Who sat there? What did you smell? What did you talk about?

At the table, I learned my values, my identity, my culture. At the kitchen table in my home, each of us five children had a seat. We lit the candles in Advent and opened the Advent calendar and sang Advent songs. Even when we came home from college, where we worshiped at St. Mattress, we still wanted to light the candles and sing the songs around the kitchen table.

At the kitchen table, over many years, the values and hopes and culture of our family were knitted together and formed in each of us. It wasn't always pleasant. When I brought home a C+ on a test, my parents did not celebrate around the table. Sometimes one of us would question the values of the table. "All the other kids can do this. Why can't I?" "You aren't all the other kids. You are a Bouman. This is what we do and don't do." "Why is my way the Bouman way?"

We told stories around the kitchen table. One day our father told us our ancestral story. He talked about his father, my grosspapa, and his immigration journey. His family were farmers. They came to this country for the same reasons immigrants and economic migrants come today. They were having trouble making ends meet and could not afford the dike taxes in the Ostfriesland part of northern Germany. This was the time of growing German imperialist ambition, the time of Bismarck and the kaiser, the late 1800s, and their neighbors were cannon fodder for wars in which they did not believe. My father told us how they sold most of their goods and heirlooms and got on a boat in Bremerhaven and crossed the Atlantic to New York. In New York they got on a train and continued the arduous journey. At midnight in Clara City, Minnesota, my grosspapa and his weary family got off the train, ended their journey, and were met by the pastor of the Lutheran church. The next day they worshiped, and after church the members, most of them farmers, met them and accompanied them to their new farm, raised their barn, and gave them the seed corn for their first harvest.

I learned about mission listening to new neighbors and making community at the kitchen table. Comparing the story of my family's welcome by the church to the experience of our new immigrant neighbors today gives me nightmares. Today we not only turn our backs on the strangers among us, we blame them!

At the kitchen table, I also got to know my biblical grandparents, Grosspapa Abraham and Grossmama Sarah, and how God's radical hospitality accompanied them on their trek as migrants from Mesopotamia to the land of Canaan. At the kitchen table, I began to learn how their story was similar to my own family's story.

For some of us, the literal kitchen table was absent; for others it was a place of bad memories or worse. But recall those places where your values, identity, and culture were formed. What were those occasions? Who was there? These relationships and interactions are your kitchen table.

Perhaps you can recall an experience like this one. I remember fishing with my grandfather, a Lutheran pastor and seminary teacher, when I was about ten years old. He looked at me and blurted out, "You know, Stephen, the only death you ever have to be afraid of is already behind you in your baptism." Then he smiled and went on fishing. What do you do with that?

When you grow up, you take it to the abyss, to your ground zero.

We saw the Twin Towers fall on 9/11. The Lutheran church in New York sustained many losses, including the parents of forty-seven children in our schools. The day after the attacks, I was at Ground Zero. I had lost my way. Staring into that obscene abyss, what my grandfather said to me came back to me as a gift: We have already been buried. The words of the apostle Paul came alive; my kitchen table was with me:

> Do you not know that all of us who have been baptized into Christ Jesus were baptized into his death? Therefore we have been buried with him by baptism into death, so that, just as Christ was raised from the dead by the glory of the Father, so we too might walk in

newness of life. For if we have been united with him in a death like his, we will certainly be united with him in a resurrection like his. (Romans 6:3-5)

Life around the kitchen table, the songs of our grandparents, the heartbeat of received story, and resurrection faith anchor us. They stay with us all our lives and come alive when we need them most. It is no accident that as we seek revival in mission as a church that is shrinking, steeped in scarcity thinking, and afraid of the future, we turn to the table to renew us.

When we talk about "tables," we do not speak of bureaucratic systems or techniques or programs. We again take our seat at the kitchen table, bathed in stories and values and rhythms of faith that have anchored us in a gracious God from generation to generation.

Visitation Stories: The Holy Is Here

When I was very small, my parents bought their first record player and two records: Bach's *Magnificat* and Rodgers and Hammerstein's *South Pacific*. They tell me that I listened to these records all the time. This was when I was just learning to speak a few words. My father says I would bound through the house singing the "Fecit Potentiam" chorus from the *Magnificat* in Latin: "He has shown strength with his arm and scattered the proud. . . ." Or all of a sudden, I would burst out with "Ain't that too damn bad!" from *South Pacific*.

Something seems right about the coupling of Mary's song with Broadway show tunes in the imagination and sensory world of a child. I didn't understand the words, but the music moved me to speech and song, as it still does. From ecstatic spiritual speech—"magnificat"—to carnal affirmation—"There is nothing like a dame"—the holy is here, in this world.

In the sixth month the angel Gabriel was sent by God to a town in Galilee called Nazareth. (Luke 1:26)

A number of years ago, I visited the Church of the Annunciation in Nazareth, the place where the angel Gabriel announced to Mary that she would "bear a son," who would "be holy . . . be called Son of God." In a crypt chapel there, carved into the altar, were the words from John's gospel: *Verbum Caro Factum Est*, "The Word became flesh."

I noticed one other little word that could only be written in that place, and it almost gave me a heart attack. "*Verbum Caro* Hic *Factum Est*." *Hic*. "Here." "Thus." The Word was made flesh here! The divine explosion of love and grace and compassion from the heart of a gracious God came *hic*—here, in the belly of this woman, Mary, in this struggling town, in this world. God enfleshed here. *Hic*.

The visitation in Mary's womb was a divine intrusion. When we receive a visitor or make a visit, we have to adjust, give space. Behind every visitation is the divine visitation of "*verbum caro factum est . . . hic,*"—right here, rearranging our priorities, quickening our hope, disrupting our patterns, deepening our compassion. In our visits with family, friends, and neighbors, every place and every conversation is holy. God is near.

Visitation makes present the "*hicness*" of God.

The presence of hope in the world, the comfort of the nearness of loved ones, the announcement of good news can only begin for us as it did for Mary. She received a visit, and then she made a visit. In the visit, God comes near. *Hic*.

> In those days Mary set out and went with haste to a Judean town in the hill country, where she entered the house of Zechariah and greeted Elizabeth. (Luke 1:39-40)

From an audience with an angel, Mary went to the kitchen table of her cousin Elizabeth. Her reaction to the promise, received in ecstatic vision from an angel and physically present in her belly, is similar to that of the shepherds and all disciples who heard angelic good news. She went in haste to share it. Like a child who does not fully know the meaning of the words yet is moved to join the melody, Mary sang along with the holy all around her. Mary's cousin Elizabeth blessed her for the child she carried in her womb and for her faith: "Blessed is the fruit of your womb. . . . Blessed is she who believed that there would be a fulfillment of what was spoken to her by the Lord" (Luke 1:42, 45).

Mary, in turn, blessed God in her song of praise: "My soul magnifies the Lord, and my spirit rejoices in God my Savior" (Luke 1:46-47). Mary translated the gospel into what it means for everyday people: the hungry, the empty, the poor. As she translated religion into life, tradition into hope, she was moving from angel's song to show tunes. She was mixing creed, "the promise he made to our ancestors, to Abraham," with human society, "from generation to generation" (vv. 55, 50). Her song is countercultural: the proud are scattered, the powerful brought down, the lowly lifted up, the hungry filled, the rich sent away empty. It is a song about what God is doing in the world—here.

Present at the visitation around the kitchen table of Elizabeth was a mute priest and father, Zechariah, who had been struck dumb for his narrow expectations of God, forced to be silent as new life began to emerge in the bellies of his wife and her cousin (see Luke 1:5-25). It gives me comfort to know that mute Zechariah was allowed to be present at the visitation, for we know that we will also be there just as we are.

Some of us have been struck mute, or something near it, by the tragic events of our time: a generation of children touched by violence in the streets of our cities; mass murders in schools, shopping malls, and movie theaters; natural disasters and ongoing wars around the world. Some of us have seen our faith and zeal slowly erode, our expectations diminish as we struggle to find our voice in a society where the love songs that once flowed from grandparent to grandchild, from generation to generation, are no longer sung. The path forward in mission will depend on a renewal of the songs of our ancestors in faith.

The Presentation: Connecting Generations and Tables

The account of the presentation of the infant Jesus at the temple in the Gospel of Luke (2:22-39) is the continuation of the incarnation of Jesus, the Word, taking on flesh in the world. The presentation at the temple gives us the wonderful image of the open, outstretched hands of an old man poised to receive and hold a baby.

Look at your hands. Can you remember holding a baby in those hands?

I recall when my hands were those of a first-time grandfather. When my first grandchild, John Paul, was born in Africa, I did not meet him until three months into his new life, except through my screensaver and pictures on the fridge. Even though I had never actually met him, I loved him and couldn't wait to hold him. As I waited by my car outside the international terminal at Kennedy airport for Timothy and Erin, my son and daughter-in-law, to carry out my grandson from Africa, my hands began to form a cradle. Then I saw them walking toward me, pulling suitcases and holding a bundle. They placed the bundle in my hands. I looked into the little face squinching from sleep toward consciousness, his tiny arms shaking. He was the conductor of my universe. John Paul. A presentation. I think I felt a little bit of what old Anna and Simeon felt as they held and beheld the infant Jesus in their hands.

Think about the hands of a mother. A few years ago, I met Father David Garcia, a priest from San Antonio, Texas, at a conference at Georgetown University. He described for me how his Mexican American community celebrates the Festival of the Presentation. The key is the hands of the mother, "La Virgen de la Candelaria," the Lady of the Candles. She holds in one hand a lighted candle; in the other, the Christ child. Themes of Epiphany light and the presentation of Jesus in the temple come together. At the Presentation Candelaria Mass, the priest blesses three things that are brought from home to church by the people.

First, the priest blesses the candles that will be used at the home altars for family devotions. It is in essence a blessing of the kitchen tables in the parish. Then he blesses the niños, which are the Christ child figures from the home crèche scenes. Often these niños are dressed lavishly. After this ceremony, they will be put away until the next Christmas season. But the Christ child continues to be present at church and at home. The presence of Christ unites the tables. Third, the priest blesses the flesh-and-blood niños and niñas, boys and girls, infants and children. The connections between the altar table and the kitchen table, between the Christ child and all children, between the church and the home and the world are beautifully woven into the celebration of Jesus' presentation.

One can imagine other congregations like this. Each sanctuary has an altar table, and beyond it are all the kitchen tables of the parish. At both tables, ancestral stories are told. At both tables, there is a seat for each member of the family by birth or baptism. Eating and drinking at each table is a united, holy thing.

The Altar Table

The altar in the church is the table that unites the kitchen tables of the congregation. Here we mark life passages as a faith community; here we bring our gifts to be shared with a wider circle. We seek to be fed and filled with spiritual food, to encounter Christ's presence and peace, to praise God, to experience loving community across the generations.

All roads meet at the altar table when the church gathers for Holy Communion. Mute, spiritually tired priests and baptized Christians; expectant believers, unseen, kicking life in the wombs of our churches; people in the breach; kin in Christ travel to the table of the Lord. There we are joined by our companions across the church, our neighbors around the corner, our singing grandparents joined with Mary and Elizabeth and their babies, angels and archangels and all the company of heaven in every time and every place.

Here, where all roads converge, we receive the dying and rising Christ, who "set out and went with haste" to visit us and all our companions on the road. *Hic.*

Consider with me the rich variety of congregational life that is brought together in the presentation story from the Gospel of Luke.

> When the time came for their purification according to the law of Moses, [Mary and Joseph] brought [Jesus] up to Jerusalem to present him to the Lord. (Luke 2:22)

The church accompanies people in the passages of their lives. In the rhythm of the parish, we are presented for baptism. The altar table joins our kitchen tables as we affirm our baptismal vows at confirmation, stand at the altar for marriage, and walk away from the altar to follow a casket to the cemetery and remember the table set among the tombstones as life goes on.

> [Mary and Joseph] offered a sacrifice according to what is stated in the law of the Lord, "a pair of turtledoves or two young pigeons." (Luke 2:24)

We all bring from our kitchen table gifts to offer to God and to the mission of the church. I have heard the church called a "charismocracy," meaning a convening of the gifts of the people. (The Greek word *charis* means "grace" or "gift of grace.") I remember growing up in a large congregation and not feeling especially involved until the years of my confirmation preparation when I was made an usher in the back balcony. I would hand out the bulletins and then, during the sermon, sit in the hallway and go through my baseball cards or read comic books. But when the music signaled the end of the sermon and the beginning of the offering, I would get my plate, collect the offering, and bring it to the altar table. Walking down the aisle to the altar, carrying my offering plate, I became a member of the church. Approaching the table with gifts was a tangible act of inclusion. At the altar table, everybody worships; everybody has something to give, a gift to offer, a way to participate.

> Now there was a man in Jerusalem whose name was Simeon; this man was righteous and devout, looking forward to the consolation of Israel. . . . It had been revealed to him by the Holy Spirit that he would not see death before he had seen the Lord's Messiah. (Luke 2:25-26)

Whether "religious" or not, every child of God is on a spiritual journey. Like Simeon, we live in great expectation and hope that our lives will mean something, that we will be fulfilled. Not every moment, not every day, but the arc of our lives bends toward consolation, reconciliation, relationship, fulfillment. The altar table is placed in the midst of such longing. Mission is also about helping each other wake up to the depth of our spiritual journeys. Everyone around the altar table is a spiritual seeker. For Simeon the promised fulfillment began when his hands gripped the baby. For us fulfillment begins as we approach the table with open hands, grasping for a bit of bread.

Simeon took [the child Jesus] in his arms and praised God. (Luke 2:28)

In a moment of spiritual clarity, Simeon embraced the promised Christ and was moved to sing, "Lord, now you let your servant depart in peace," the Nunc dimittis. The words of a sermon, the testimony of a lay leader, the presence of family sitting around you as you sing a beloved hymn, a visit when you are in the hospital, an insight in a Bible study—there are moments when Jesus is real and present and brings peace beyond words. The Holy Spirit's presence animates life around the tables. We glimpse that first table in the midst of creation. As for Simeon, the spiritual clarity moves us to witness and testimony and song.

But not always.

As Simeon presented his song, his gaze fell on the child's mother, and his voice struck a minor key. In the midst of fulfillment, he saw Mary's impending grief. He acknowledged a place at the table for sadness, grief, incomprehension. His spiritual expression embraced solidarity with a mother who would suffer: "A sword will pierce your own soul" (Luke 2:35).

Think of that piercing sword in your soul and in the soul of the alcoholic who can't make it another day, the wife whose husband is leaving her, the father who cannot speak to his teenage child anymore, the person with the shocking diagnosis, the provider who lost a job, the sister whose dark night of the soul seems to go on forever, the grieving widow so lonely she says she would speak to the devil if she could. Think of how your place at the table is a place of comfort and hope, or maybe just presence in the midst of daily life.

There was also a prophet, Anna the daughter of Phanuel, of the tribe of Asher. She was of a great age, having lived with her husband seven years after her marriage, then as a widow to the age of eighty-four. She never left the temple but worshiped there with fasting and prayer night and day. (Luke 2:36-37)

It seems only fitting that Anna, who has been in the altar guild for a good portion of her eighty-four years, shows up in this narrative. God is also placed in her hands. Church is one of the few places in our society in which gifts and relationship can be shared across the generations.

The Annas of our churches keep the oral history of the congregation, and they are the most open to change for the sake of mission and are personally involved in hospitality and communal pastoral care ministries. In the congregations I served, they conversed with the Korean group and with other immigrants, helping them practice their English. They got to know the young children in our early childhood school and their families.

The Annas of the congregation of my youth helped me learn to worship. My mother sat with us five kids every Sunday (my father had the easier job as the organist and choir director). She would bribe us with Froot Loops and books and toys to earn our relative silence. When we got really restive, the woman behind us would give us Chiclets. We called her the gum lady. Then would come the time for my mother, the gum lady, and our elders to go to the altar to receive communion. We were abandoned in the pew. But we paid attention. When my mother came back, she was different. She looked different. She smelled different. From watching my elders take communion, I learned things about the holy that I could never learn in a Sunday school class. At the altar, the kitchen table of our church, was a community of mentors, people who helped us find jobs as we grew older and who asked about our lives when we came home from college. They were the Annas and Simeons of our life journeys.

From the kitchen table, we are sent to the altar table, and from there into the world as story and sign bearers of the Creator's vision for reconciliation, forgiveness, restoration, and grace. In the next chapter, we will see the rhythm of mission as the leaving of our tables to seek company at the tables in our communities and world.

Read and Reflect, Discuss and Reflect

1. Read Luke 1:39-55 and Luke 2:22-39. What do the passages say to you, at this time and place, about God, the church, and the wider world?
2. The Word became flesh and dwelled among us. Where have you experienced God dwelling in your life? Share your experience.
3. Not everyone has experienced a "kitchen table" as described in this chapter. Where was the place where you learned your values, your

identity, your culture? Who were some of the people who taught you these things?

4. What relationships across generations are evident in your congregation?

5. What stories or love songs does your congregation tell or sing about how God has been and is at work among you?

CHAPTER 3

Seeking Hospitality
at New Tables

[Jesus] came down with them and stood on a level place, with a great crowd of his disciples and a great multitude of people from all Judea, Jerusalem, and the coast of Tyre and Sidon. They had come to hear him and to be healed of their diseases; and those who were troubled with unclean spirits were cured. And all in the crowd were trying to touch him, for power came out from him and healed all of them. Then he looked up at his disciples and said:

> *"Blessed are you who are poor,*
>   *for yours is the kingdom of God.*
> *"Blessed are you who are hungry now,*
>   *for you will be filled.*
> *"Blessed are you who weep now,*
>   *for you will laugh."*

—Luke 6:17-21

The Gospel of Luke puts Jesus' great sermon on the plain, the "level place." The table moves closer to the people, and poverty becomes literal, not just spiritualized as in "Blessed are the poor in spirit" (Matthew 5:3).

Imagine Jesus teaching about the reign of God as a stone thrown in the water, causing waves to ripple out in concentric circles. His message was "Blessed are you who are poor, for yours is the kingdom of God" (Luke 6:20).

After preaching about mission, Jesus put legs on the sermon and lived it. Scripture says, "After Jesus had finished all his sayings in the hearing of the people, he entered Capernaum" (Luke 7:1). In Capernaum words became deeds. Jesus backed up his teaching with actions that crossed boundaries and engaged the most vulnerable: a centurion's servant and the widow at Nain. He repeated his vision for the reign of God and its mission to John's disciples, saying, "Tell John what you have seen and heard" (Luke 7:22). He described to them a mission of restoration and reconciliation in which the blind see, the lame walk, lepers are cleansed, the deaf hear, the dead are raised, and the poor have good news brought to them.

Jesus taught then acted, giving the message integrity through his actions. Recall the story in Mark 2 about the four people carrying a paralyzed man to Jesus for healing. Jesus was teaching about the forgiveness of sins and then credentialed his message by healing the paralytic. Here is what happened when the reign of God came near, when the teachings of Jesus were enacted: a paralytic was carried into the house (through the roof), but he walked out.

What would that look like in your church and your community?

Jesus Sent Companions Seeking Hospitality

Now see the ripples move even farther outward. In Luke 8 we see the mission expand, leadership expand, and the communal servants of the mission grew and were challenged and inspired by the *accompaniment* of Jesus. Jesus continued to act on his teachings, but now he intentionally took people with him, teaching by example and preparing them for their roles. Every mission leader is both apprentice and mentor.

> Soon afterwards [Jesus] went on through cities and villages, proclaiming and bringing the good news of the kingdom of God. The twelve were with him, as well as some women who had been cured of evil

spirits and infirmities: Mary, called Magdalene . . . Joanna . . . and Susanna, and many others. (Luke 8:1-3)

This is learning through doing and then reflecting on what has occurred. Jesus engaged the Twelve and also three women who were wounded healers. He was teaching them by example and taking them with him. The circles rippled farther outward.

What might this "action-reflection accompaniment" look like in the life of a congregation? Let me share one example. In many churches, each year at Christmas youth groups go caroling, often to homebound members or nursing homes. The next time your group goes to a nursing home, don't send the young people home afterward. Gather and reflect on the experience. Ask some questions: What did you hear? What did you smell? What were you thinking and feeling? What did you see in the faces? Let them talk about what they have just gone through. Then read the story in Luke 2 of the presentation of Jesus, and talk about Simeon and Anna. This kind of activity teaches through acting and reflecting on what has been done, and this is what Jesus did with his followers in Luke's gospel.

In Luke 9 the ripples continue to flow outward. There Jesus takes the training wheels off the bicycle of mission. Now you go do it.

> Then Jesus called the twelve together and gave them power and authority over all demons and to cure diseases, and he sent them out to proclaim the kingdom of God and to heal. He said to them, "Take nothing for your journey, no staff, nor bag, nor bread, nor money. . . . Whatever house you enter, stay there, and leave from there. . . ." They departed and went through the villages, bringing the good news and curing diseases everywhere. (Luke 9:1-6)

Do you notice the stance of this communal band of missionary leaders? They travel light. They leave behind the props of their daily existence—staff, bag, money, bread. They leave their own table and go forth into the community as vulnerable guests finding themselves at the kitchen tables of their neighbors, eating what is put in front of them.

Mission is the seeking of hospitality at the tables of our neighbors in the world, seeking a welcome. We don't approach our neighbors primarily to catalog and meet their needs. God is already there. Great competence and giftedness are already present. We go to listen to the stories of our new hosts at the table, to receive their welcome, and if invited, to tell our own story. We are seeking to be partners, communal artisans for new space and the creation of new tables. We understand that in the storytelling, invitations, and hospitality, all of our tables will be renewed, transformed, repurposed. Community is those who throw their lot in with each other and who know who the others are. Community brings accountability, and so needs will be met, but the terms of engagement are the ethics and vision of the mutual table.

I find it striking that in Jesus' instructions in Luke 9 (and also in Luke 10) he explicitly commands the visitors not to bring bread with them. Why is that? Well, what did you learn at your kitchen table about what you do when you eat at someone else's house as a guest? "Eat what they put in front of you." We do not bring bread because we will eat the bread of our hosts. We are guests. We become *companions* with those with whom we share bread. In Spanish, Latin, and French, the root words for *companion* are *con* ("with") and *pan* ("bread"). And in the bread sharing, we all become companions with Jesus, the ultimate host at every table. Mission is eucharist.

Next the ripples of mission engage all of us. In Luke 10, the fledgling mission cadre expands. There the Lord appointed the Seventy (that's all of us!) and sent them on ahead of him to every town and place *he intended to go* (v. 1).

> He said to them, "The harvest is plentiful, but the laborers are few; therefore ask the Lord of the harvest to send out laborers into his harvest." (Luke 10:2)

Again Jesus joined those he sent as a mission community seeking hospitality and welcome in the world. He sent them two by two as companions seeking companions. In sending the Twelve, the women who were wounded healers, and the Seventy (two by two), Jesus was showing us something of the vocation for human beings in this world. The church is a community of companions—bread sharers—seeking and sharing the companionship of Jesus for the life of the world.

Mission as Visitation on the Road

Each of the visitations Jesus inaugurated in Luke 6–10 is meant to be a gracious expression of our companionship and kinship in Christ. In chapter 2, we considered the kitchen table of Elizabeth, and we remembered our own cultural and spiritual formation *around* the kitchen table. Now let's consider *the journey to and from* the tables. Mary's heart was so full with the angelic announcement that she had to be with kin. She set out on the road "with haste" and urgency. The little detail that she went to "a Judean town in the hill country" (1:39) is worth repeating. The road to connect with kin was long and arduous for a newly pregnant woman. In the way of Jesus, relationship is everything.

Mary's visitation on parched and devastated roads must have taken much effort. This is also true in the visitations of missional listening in our ministry today. Behind the difficult journeys and the improvised roads has been the faith that this mutual connecting on the road is worth it, that the resolve to stay connected is somehow as central to our spiritual values and life of faith as that of a pregnant woman setting out through the hill country to visit her pregnant kin.

Standing on the ridge of the mountain in Tanzania where the Ruhija Seminary, African Arts and Music School is located, one can look down into the valley below. One sees the smoke from cooking fires, the lush green of the banana and coffee shambas (fields), clusters of huts, goats, and other signs of life lived pretty close to the bone. No electricity, running water, or major roads are in the near future in this valley. And one can see crisscrossing the shambas and connecting the lone huts and village clusters, a network of paths cut into the dense foliage. These paths are life itself for those who live here.

Along these paths in Ruhija, midwives travel to deliver babies, mourners travel with comfort for the bereaved, food travels to the market, the hungry and lonely are visited with bread and company, the isolated hut is connected to news and gossip, lovers meet, dusty young feet trudge to school, medicine is brought to the sick, the evangelist arrives at a hut to lead a village Bible study, the pastor brings the Eucharist to the aged and sick, help arrives to pick the harvest, and the person dying of AIDS or malaria receives visitors who hold off the final loneliness.

Think of the human longing for companionship and holiness expressed in these roads and pathways. Think of the spring in the step of Mary, belly swollen, heading for the kitchen table of her cousin. Think of the flooded sanctuaries in Minot, North Dakota, or Staten Island, New York, where roads of rescue and comfort intersect; of Ground Zero and the incredible paths forged for rescue and recovery. Can we see our families, friends, congregations, and church bodies as a series of roads and pathways connecting us to one another and the grace all around us? We are kin in Christ.

Sent from the Table

The root of the word *religion* means literally "to connect again": *re* = "again"; *ligione* (ligament) = "to connect." The root of *synod* is similar, literally "together on the road" (*syn* + *hodos*). The shrinking church has been stuck at its own tables, losing its connection to the tables of its community. Renewal in mission involves leaving our table and seeking companionship at new tables, our neighbors' tables, living and sharing the story of the death and resurrection of Jesus for the life of the world.

Congregations across many denominations are seeking ways to engage their communities, joining God's restoring and reconciling mission in the world. Many examples bear witness to how congregations are leaving their own tables and seeking companionship at new tables.

❊ ❊ ❊

St. Luke's, in Farmingdale, Long Island, left the church table and entered the community in search of hospitality among their new Latino neighbors. With the leadership of a Spanish-speaking deacon, a team from the congregation listened to the community by having one-on-one conversations with over one hundred Latino residents. In Laundromats, in restaurant kitchens, in bodegas, and on street corners, they listened and learned about the lives of their neighbors: their hopes and dreams, their networks of support, their places of need and great giftedness. In the listening, new relationships began to be knitted together and a new table began to emerge.

In the very act of listening, gifts of grace and good news were given and received. When St. Luke's had their initial liturgy in Spanish on Easter Sunday, the large attendance was the fruit of this listening. The congregation's altar table was renewed, enlarged in scope and imagination.

In a congregation I served as pastor in New Jersey, an eighty-year-old lifelong member of our church and community, Agnes, caused us to leave the altar table and move toward the community. She lived alone in an old frame house. She had no place to go where she could continue some measure of independent living. There were no affordable housing options in our part of North Jersey for older adults on fixed incomes. We had helped her search for over a year. Her home and her inner and outer health deteriorated badly. She died when her house burned down. The following year, with Agnes on our hearts, during the Week of Prayer for Christian Unity, the leaders of the congregations in our community resolved to interview every older adult living alone in our town. A nun trained a group of us in holding one-on-one conversations with our neighbors. More than 250 elderly neighbors told us what Agnes had already taught us: affordable housing was their primary concern. An ecumenical committee was formed to research and advocate for housing options. New tables were coming into view. We successfully negotiated with private and public sector leaders and achieved an accessory housing ordinance that would enable the renovation of a property for the creation of an additional affordable housing unit for low-income seniors. We gained seventy new units of affordable housing. These new tables of ecumenical engagement in the public arena and relationship building with our older adult neighbors revitalized our congregation and its members. Our embrace of our community and its most vulnerable neighbors was a reason we added many new members to our altar table.

Congregations across the ELCA are bringing creative missional imagination to strategies for their future. At the 2011 churchwide assembly of the ELCA, every congregation was invited to engage in a time of discerning and discovering their mission strategy. It was an invitation to renew the congregation table and its disciples as they dreamed and planned for setting new tables in the midst of the world. Renewing the congregation's connection to its community is critical to this process.

Many rural congregations in the Southwestern Minnesota Synod are doing this discernment together, identifying where they see opportunities as neighbors to plan mission and pastoral care together. This synod is encouraging the process of "courtship," "engagement," and "marriage" for mission in the creation of these multi-table parishes.

More than half of the new mission starts in the ELCA between 2008 and 2013 have been with immigrant communities, among ethnic-specific populations, or in contexts of deep poverty. These tables are set by listening, creating and strengthening relationships, sharing gifts, and bearing one another's burdens.

❖ ❖ ❖

The Welcome Church in Philadelphia is a ministry not only *for* but *of* homeless people and people in poverty. It began when Pastor Violet Little and some of the members of the Welcome Church left the altar table in their sanctuary to begin worship with homeless people at a train station in Philadelphia. The ministry has become an ecumenical, multisite expression of God's renewing and restoring grace. This ministry and twelve others like it across the country—called "Jesus and justice" ministries—use the gifts of leaders from these communities and have formed a group for mutual support and leadership development.

The Leaven Project is a new mission table being set on the east side of Portland, Oregon, to engage young adults, most of whom have lost touch with or never had any connection to traditional congregation tables. This "emergent" outreach has two leaders who are also young adults: Melissa Reed, a mission developer pastor, and Wendy Hall, a community organizer. This ministry is supported and housed as an investment in the future by Redeemer Lutheran Church, a vital urban congregation with a dwindling membership but expansive vision. Redeemer has "left the table" to enable the formation of new tables. Some who participate speak the name of Jesus with abiding faith; others would never have been caught dead near an institutional church until their encounter with the Leaven Project. Prayers, personal testimonies, and candle lighting give liturgical rhythm and connection to a community moored and tethered to the narrative of Jesus and the church of the ages. A cohort of fifteen such ELCA ministries across the country staffed by young mission developers and community organizers has formed for mutual support, training, and resolve to multiply their number. Their leaders meet together regularly, challenge and support each other, and have been mentors for many other young adult leaders and emergent ministries across the church. And there are many small yet vibrant congregations like Redeemer, midwives of the Leaven Project, who have this resolve: If we are going to go down, let us go down serving.

Come with me to visit the Leaven Project in Portland and see how the tables merge into one another: the project releases leaders into the community as members of a church-based community organization. On the day I visited them, these leaders were returning from a meeting with city officials concerning the city's budget and projected cuts in services to the most vulnerable people. From this table rooted in the wider community, they returned to their church table. Over thirty of us sat in a circle as the leaders evaluated the action with the city officials, their own performance and meeting of their goals, as well as their sense of the meaning of what they were trying to accomplish.

As they shared their hopes for the city and its most vulnerable people, the public table began to morph into an altar. They welcomed me and engaged me in a conversation about my journey as a pastor and leader in community organizing. Then candles were distributed and the liturgy began. Each person gave a statement about his or her life and hopes for the coming week and then lit a candle and placed it in a tub of sand in our midst. This was a time of sharing joys and challenges. After listening in the wider community, they were now listening to one another at their faith table. In all of it, they were struggling to listen to God's presence, wisdom, and direction. Some spoke direct words of praise and faith in Jesus' presence in their lives. Some lamented the absence of God in their lives but expressed gratitude for the community. Their communal narrative came alive before my eyes, an emergent table of grace.

From our kitchen tables, God calls us to meet Christ at the altar table. From the altar table, we are sent to gather at the tables of neighbors and set new tables with new friends. Mission is moving from table to table, seeking to join God already in the world making new space for reconciling, renewing grace.

Read and Reflect, Discuss and Reflect

1. Read Luke 6:17—9:6 and Luke 10:1-12. What do the passages say to you, at this time and place, about God, the church, and the wider world?

2. Think about a time when someone mentored you in a new task or skill. What was it? How did it go? In what ways did it involve action and reflection? Who accompanied you?

3. What actions and activities in the community is your congregation currently carrying out? Do they include a time of participants' reflection on the activity? If not, where might you start?

4. Who are your neighbors where you live? Who are your congregation's neighbors? In what ways do you come together as companions? What are the paths and roads in your community that connect you—common activities and interests, special events, community causes, and improvement projects?

CHAPTER 4

The Congregation: A Table for Mission

Day by day, as they spent much time together in the temple, they broke bread at home and ate their food with glad and generous hearts, praising God and having the goodwill of all the people. And day by day the Lord added to their number those who were being saved.

—Acts 2:46-47

In this chapter, we will go deep in seeking a biblical arc that shapes the congregation's *mission table*, which connects the kitchen tables of its members at the altar table and sends its people out to new tables of God's restoring and reconciling mission. The ELCA Book of Faith Initiative, which seeks to reconnect the church with the Bible, invites us to "open Scripture" and "join the conversation." We open and read the Bible together around the table to be inspired, to get in touch with the passion of Jesus' love for the world, and for wisdom guiding the aspirations we have for our lives and congregations. As a congregation begins to embrace its opportunities for mission, it can begin to develop a selection of Bible stories that have power to inspire people with God's past faithfulness and illumine present possibilities. This is where the Book of Faith joins the mission table.

Ten Biblical Marks of a Missional Congregation

We will explore ten marks of a missional congregation that grow out of scripture's testimony:

1. A congregation in mission is always listening.
2. A congregation in mission mentors and trains its leaders.
3. A congregation in mission nurtures communal leadership.
4. A congregation in mission faces paralysis with courage.
5. A congregation in mission reroots in its community.
6. A congregation in mission risks new things.
7. A congregation in mission makes all decisions based on its mission.
8. A congregation in mission is clear about money and relationships.
9. A congregation in mission is propelled by the resurrection of Jesus.
10. A congregation in mission is shaped by Word and sacraments.

1. A congregation in mission is always listening.

Trace the arc of Jesus and listening in the Gospel of Luke. It begins with Jesus as a boy in the temple listening to his elders in the faith. "After three days they found him in the temple, sitting among the teachers, listening to them and asking them questions" (Luke 2:46). From the very beginning, Jesus was always listening to others, drawing out their spiritual hunger, responding with love and grace and truth. But mostly in Luke's gospel people don't listen to Jesus.

He reads the scriptures in his home church in Galilee, connecting his mission with the Servant Song in Isaiah. The hometown crowd won't listen. "Isn't this Mary and Joe's kid? Who does he think he is, anyway?" Luke says, "They got up, drove him out of the town, and led him to the brow of the hill on which their town was built, so that they might hurl him off the cliff" (Luke 4:29). His home congregation didn't listen.

But people begin to notice him and are drawn to his public teaching and healing ministry in his home region of Galilee. Luke records, "Now more than ever the word about Jesus spread abroad; many crowds would gather to hear him and to be cured of their diseases" (Luke 5:15). The Jewish leaders come up from Jerusalem to check out this Jesus. They are not impressed. "Who does he think he is—the Messiah?" "Then the scribes and the Pharisees began to question, 'Who is this who is speaking blasphemies? Who can forgive sins but God alone?'" (Luke 5:21).

Jesus has a moment when he really thinks that the disciples are listening to him. "Once when Jesus was praying alone, with only the disciples near him, he asked them, 'Who do the crowds say that I am?' They answered, 'John the Baptist; but others, Elijah; and still others, that one of the ancient prophets has arisen.' He said to them, 'But who do you say that I am?' Peter answered, 'The Messiah of God'" (Luke 9:18-20). It seems Peter has been listening.

And one day, like a small miracle, Jesus dines with friends and someone just sits down and listens to him: "[Martha] had a sister named Mary, who sat at the Lord's feet and listened to what he was saying" (Luke 10:39). Mary listened, and her listening enabled Jesus to speak. What did he say? What did she hear? We aren't told, but in the context of the deaf ears in Luke's gospel, we can assume that Mary's listening was a graceful thing, an occasion for Jesus to unfold some of his story and its passions with another human being. Martha, like the busy pastor rushing around the church and the neighborhood, had important things to do. They remain important. But maybe, like Mary's listening to Jesus, the most important miracles in congregations have their genesis in the silence and attentiveness of human conversation.

The most effective mission strategies I have encountered have not been the ones with all the demographic bells and whistles and the embodiment of the latest process and strategic theories. They have been about congregations really caring and creating space and hospitality for the stories of their members and neighbors to be told. As it was for Jesus, to be in mission is to listen.

In the story of Mary and Martha, we see the listening of Mary in the context of the table of hospitality that Martha was setting. Listening sets new tables by enabling new relationships, and it undergirds the mission of a church and community. Luke takes us from Mary's listening to the next chapter where the hunger of the disciples to listen to God comes into view: "Lord, teach us to pray" (Luke 11:1).

A congregation in mission is always *listening*.

2. A congregation in mission mentors and trains its leaders.

I've begun to read Matthew 14:13-33 as a mentoring story. Jesus had just heard about the death of John the Baptist. Fully human like us, he needed to withdraw to a lonely place to absorb the news and grieve. The ebb and flow of daily life often confounds those who mourn. I remember walking out of the hospital after watching a loved one die. I hit the busy streets thinking, *How can you all go about your business like any other day? Don't you know what just happened in there?*

At the intersection of his grief and the daily crush of the crowds, Jesus had compassion and listened to the people and healed their sick. Then as the evening came and the hunger of a long day took hold of the crowd he had been teaching, Jesus set a table and mentored his disciples. "You give them something to eat," Jesus said to them (Matthew 14:16), seizing on this teaching moment. He set a table in the tension of scarcity and abundance, just as we come to the tables of our kitchens and congregations in the midst of that tension. He received the gifts of loaves and fishes, which came from the crowd. His example teaches: Don't be afraid of the crowd. Attend to their great hunger of body and soul but also their giftedness. Their loaves and fishes count for something. When Jesus sets the table, gifts multiply; there is always enough.

Then it was night, and the grieving hunger in Jesus cried out for a hearing. We read, "He made the disciples get into the boat and go on ahead to the other side, while he dismissed the crowds. And after he had dismissed the crowds, he went up on the mountain by himself to pray. When evening came, he was there alone" (Matthew 14:22-23).

Now let's think about congregations, synods, and denominations and the church's many fears about an unknown future. Imagine we are in the boat with the disciples in roiling water; the wind is in our faces; and it is "early in the morning" (Matthew 14:25), literally "the fourth watch" of the night, between

3:00 and 6:00 in the morning. The fourth watch is the bewitching hour, a time when all we fear, can't see, and can't control is running amuck. Now imagine this: right into the primal fear and upwind resistance and stormy terror of the unknown comes Jesus, walking on water, moving toward us.

The biblical account tells us that Peter wanted to leave the boat and move toward the Jesus future. I read this more and more as a leadership mentoring story. Jesus was never more a teacher and coach than when he invited Peter out of the safety of the boat. With one word Jesus committed to a future leader: "Come."

A missional congregation invests in leaders and has a plan for leadership development. The congregation sees everything it does as opportunity for leadership development. A time of mission strategy and discernment can be an opportunity to develop the gifts and passions of people.

- Who is inviting the next generation of the church's and community's spiritual seekers and leaders out of the boat these days?
- Who is setting tables for their collaboration?
- Is church a place where the development of the faith and competence of its leaders is the highest priority?
- Is your church a place that represents the safety of the boat or the scary, exhilarating invitation to walk on water?

Jesus said to Peter, "Come."

3. A congregation in mission nurtures communal leadership.

In Exodus 2:11-12 we read that Moses killed an Egyptian who was beating a Hebrew. The traditional interpretation of this story is that when Moses saw that the coast was clear—"he looked this way and that"—he went ahead and killed the oppressor of his people. But Hillel, a rabbi and contemporary of Jesus, offered another opinion. He said that Moses was looking for help. He looked left and right, and when he saw that he was alone, he reluctantly fought and did what he had to do.

Hillel believed that the rest of the Hebrew scriptures are about this story, *about the building of community* so that Moses and Israel would never again be in the position where "he looked this way and that way, and [saw] no one . . ." And indeed the Passover narrative is about a motley group of slaves coming through the sea and the wilderness and becoming a people with a communal identity. In addition, it seems that Moses' father-in-law, Jethro, tried to help Moses be a better community organizer and argued for communal leadership (Exodus 18:18-23). "Are you nuts, Moses, trying to discern the issues of everyone all at once all by yourself? Why don't you organize with a team of leaders, each one to judge over one hundred." Verse 24 says that "Moses listened to his father-in-law and did all that he had said," and over the course of their forty-year wilderness trek, the Israelites were formed into a community with a team of leaders.

Jerome, who lived in the fourth century AD, said, "*Ecclesia non est quae habet sacerdotes,*" which translates roughly, "There can be no church community without a leader or team of leaders." I believe that mission today will be led by teams of leaders with a deep reservoir of gifts and talents that build up the leadership of the body of Christ. Leadership takes its cue from the apostle Paul: one body, many members.

In his book *Reclaiming the Great Commission,* Episcopal bishop Claude Payne talks about "total ministry," which exists where the pastoral leadership of the congregation belongs to the whole community and there is a commitment to the development of a strong collective of lay leaders.[3] Congregations are enriched by lay leaders, many of whose leadership has been formed in the lifelong learning centers across the country, such as the various synod Lay Schools of Theology or a nationwide program like Diakonia. Some of these leaders have come out of certificate programs for youth and family ministry. I see a proliferation of such certificate programs in the future: steward leadership, community organizing, lay evangelism, and as many others as the contexts and missional needs lead us to imagine.

In Tanzania, in even the remotest places, congregations have teams of leaders and an infrastructure for mission in place. There are local evangelists (usually spiritual leaders who come from the community), catechists, deaconesses, social ministry organizations like dispensaries, trained musicians, and many other leaders. The pastor may cover several congregations within the parish, but the local church has a cadre of leaders in place to sustain and grow the ministry.

Whether in rural North Dakota or in urban situations like the South Bronx, the trend for lay and pastoral leadership will continue to be toward homegrown leaders. Immigrant congregations are sending out teams of lay leaders to begin new Latino mission starts in Florida and Los Angeles and many other places, for example. Where mission flourishes, leadership multiplies.

4. A congregation in mission faces paralysis with courage.

John 5:1-9 tells the story of Jesus showing up at the hour of worship in Jerusalem. At that place was a pool called Bethesda, and near it, in the narthex (five of them actually), lay many invalids—blind, lame, paralyzed—on their mats. It was a kind of Darwinian system of health care—those with the means, with the help, with the right connections, resources, or friends got to the pool. One man had been lying on his mat in sight of the healing pool for thirty-eight years but was always a day late and a dollar short.

"When Jesus saw him lying there and knew that he had been there a long time, he said to him, 'Do you want to be made well?'" (John 5:6). Jesus noticed the suffering and helplessness. He "knew he had been there a long time." Jesus always shows up at the place of deepest vulnerability. We hear echoes of the voice speaking to Moses from the bush: "I have observed the misery of my people. . . . I know their sufferings" (Exodus 3:7). God has noticed the suffering in our many tragedies. God wants to be in the breach with us.

But why did Jesus ask the question he asked: "Do you want to be made well?" He stood before someone chronically ill, lame, unable to walk for thirty-eight years. Why ask such a person that question? It sounds insensitive, almost like a taunt. You can almost hear the man grumble to himself, "Well, what do you think?"

The question roused the man to a spirited response. He was just lying there, but now he was animated, ticked. He spit out his anger: "Sir, I have no one to put me into the pool when the water is stirred up; and while I am making my way, someone else steps down ahead of me" (John 5:7).

Why, indeed, would Jesus ask this man, "Do you want to be made well?" It is the only question that matters. If the man doesn't want to be made well, he will continue to make a life for himself sitting by the side of the pool. Our pathologies can domesticate us.

All of us, sisters and brothers, are on our mats. All of us are at the many tables of the church together. Do we want to be made well? It's the only question for congregations stalled in their ministry, timid in their stewardship, lax in their discipleship, stifled in their imagination about the future, afraid of the changing communities outside their doors.

It is the only question for those who have endured tragedy and resent the whole world moving on while they are stuck. "You, heart closed, turned inward, still seething, paralyzed by what happened, do you really want to be made well?"

It's the only question for a world paralyzed by anger, sitting beside the pool on the mat of its many divisions. Do we really want to be made well? Individually, in our congregations, in our relationships—do we really want to be made well, or will we clutch our rationalizations, our fears, our addictions, and our self-delusions and self-absorption and talk about why we never get to the pool? Will we stop trying to drag ourselves to the pool we know we will never reach long enough to notice the Healer standing in our midst?

Jesus said to the sick man, "Stand up, take your mat and walk" (John 5:8). Jesus did not touch him or put him in the water. Even the word for "rise" (NRSV "stand up") in the Greek is a reflexive verb, which means the subject (the man) is also the object of the verb *rise*. You can't raise someone else; you can only raise yourself.

The man by the pool was caught in a thirty-eight-year cycle of apathy and anger. The root meaning for the Old Norse word *angr* is grief. It is mourning the distance between what was and what has become; it is grief over the distance between what is and what ought to be. Jesus found a man disabled in more ways than physically. He was apathetic (from the Greek *a-pathos*, "without feeling"). Jesus' question stirred him to grieving anger.

We will never move into new tables in mission while renewing our own congregational tables in ways that heal and serve until we get in touch with our anger and shout it out in exorcising grief. We need to unleash the lamentations stuck in our throats.

- "This is supposed to be a place of healing, and no one helps me!"
- "For thirty-eight years nobody who made it to the pool came back to help me!"
- "People pushed me away, ran over me!"
- "I didn't ask to be born this way; why will no one welcome me to the healing pool?"
- "Where was God on September 11, 2001? On December 14, 2012, in Newtown, Connecticut?"
- "Why did God take my buddy in the firehouse and leave me?"
- "Why aren't our children in church anymore?"

Our individual lives and our life together are riddled with grieving anger between what was and what has become, between what is and what ought to be.

- "This is my Father's house, and you have made it a den of thieves."
- "Our country welcomed my grandparents, and today we not only hate strangers but blame them."
- "Why does my congregation seem so joyless?"
- "Why am I so stuck in my dreams and in my faith? Nothing seems to be going anywhere!"
- "Why does an equitable society seem so impossible to achieve?"

This kind of anger about what is and what ought to be will move our values. It can break our hearts open again. God can work with this kind of grief. Do you want to be made well? In your life? Your church? Your community? Then stand up! Get up!

But then in the biblical story Jesus does something else that jars us. Once the man has stood up, he is finally free to walk after thirty-eight years and is about to take the first step into unencumbered freedom. And then Jesus says, "Take your mat" (John 5:8). Jesus makes him take up his mat. Why?

Think about it. Why does someone who hasn't taken a drink for ten years still call himself an alcoholic? In the story, the healing by the pool led to testimony. The mat became the man's history of God's healing providence. We have to connect our hope with our history. Those who are healed have a story to tell about where and who they have been. The call to healing is a call not to leave our mats behind or pretend they are not there. We are dragging mats on our collective backs as we attempt to rise up as a church in mission.

The call to healing does not make light of the divisions among us, of what our congregation has been through, of what we have lost. It is a call to walk away from apathy and also from hot anger. It is a call to cool "*angr,*" the grief of the gulf between what was and what has become, between what is and what should be. It is a holy longing to be well. It is a resolve to turn our gaze from the pool that is reflecting back our paralysis and apathy and to look into the eyes of Jesus standing with us in our paralysis—Jesus, the one who calls us to the place of anger transformed to healing grace for the life of the world.

5. A congregation in mission reroots in its community.

In the healing story from Matthew 9:18-26, Jesus was in the middle of teaching his disciples and some disciples of John the Baptist when the synagogue leader (called Jairus in Mark's and Luke's accounts) interrupted Jesus—and Jesus allowed himself to be interrupted: "While he was saying these things to them, suddenly a leader of the synagogue came in and knelt before him, saying, 'My daughter has just died; but come and lay your hand on her, and she will live'" (v. 18).

Interruptions. The parish ministries in which I served were always with immigrant people, with people in poverty with busy and difficult lives with many interruptions—visas, immigration documents, ill family members back in the home country, job losses, apartment hunting, issues with the children and families. The door of a congregation must always be open to the community, because, remember, Jesus allowed himself to be interrupted.

"And Jesus got up and followed him, with his disciples" (Matthew 9:19). Jesus did not attend to the task at hand alone, and neither should a pastor. Ministry is the business of all disciples. One mark of a congregation in mission is collective leadership, "total ministry" (see point 3 above). So Jesus

'open' inward + 'open' outward

let a desperate father change his agenda and direct his steps. But before Jesus could make this home visit with his disciples, there was another interruption, and Jesus again let someone else's need change his plans. "Suddenly a woman who had been suffering from hemorrhages for twelve years came up behind him" (Matthew 9:20).

What follows in the story from Matthew is an anatomy of an emerging mission table. By being out and about with the disciples, Jesus made himself and his companions "touchable" for the life of the community to flow to them and through them. For twelve long years, this woman had been "untouchable," a pariah. She was barred from every table. For twelve long years, she could not sit at the table of worship or the kitchen table of family. She had to keep her distance from everybody. She lived on the fringe of society, barren, untouched, alone.

Who are those people in your community, your society? Maybe on some days it is you who can feel some of what that woman felt being on the outside, vulnerable, despised, and sometimes invisible.

Matthew says, "[She] came up behind him and touched the fringe of his cloak, for she said to herself, 'If I only touch his cloak, I will be made well.'" This took much courage. Her going out in public and being near other people was a violation of purity laws. Touching a man, touching a holy man, even touching the fringe of his clothing was utterly forbidden. But she did it anyway. She did not put herself in Jesus' path, and she did not call out his name. She just reached for the fringe, to touch . . . something.

Think of how much courage it takes to enter someone else's church, job, or community. Many people who approach the church today or are seeking Jesus or even a small sign of hope only dare approach on the edges. The alcoholic, the person whose family is breaking up, the person whose mother is dying, the person lonely for the home country—so many have reasons to approach the fringe of Jesus' presence. Human hunger seeks a place at the table. Being a little ashamed or feeling unworthy, still the spiritually hungry take a courageous step toward Jesus—coming quietly to church one day and sitting in the back or calling the pastor when things become too hard or too sad.

With one courageous step, the sick woman took a chance on Jesus, but everything depended on his response. "Jesus turned, and seeing her he said, 'Take heart, daughter; your faith has made you well' " (Matthew 9:22). In this short sentence, Jesus made three astonishing moves toward setting a table between them. First, Jesus turned and saw her. We need churches and ministries that turn toward people in need and really see them. He saw her because he was there to see her. He was in her neighborhood. He was in her path. The fringe of his garment was within reach so that when she stretched out her hand, she touched Jesus, not thin air. How can our congregations locate their life and presence in the pain and hunger and life of their communities so that their neighbors can touch the fringe of the body of Christ? Jesus turned and saw *her*. Not a statistic. Not a stereotype. Not a label. Not a budget item. Not an "immigrant." Just her.

Second, Jesus called her "daughter." There was no wall between them. No separation. "Take heart, daughter," he said, as though she were his own flesh and blood. He recognized her pain as his own. In calling the woman "daughter," was Jesus also channeling the desperate love of the father who asked him to heal his daughter? When someone touches the hem of the body of Christ, he or she becomes kin and renews the table of the congregation.

Third, Jesus saw her giftedness, her human dignity, and said, "Your faith has made you well" (Matthew 9:22). Jesus saw her, called her "daughter," and lifted up her giftedness, and she rose up, a witness to the faith. Rerooting the life of the congregation in its community is an invitation to reset its mission within the great giftedness of its neighbors, within renewed relationships where strangers become kin, within hopeful healing possibilities around new tables. It begins with noticing and listening and then fostering a communal leadership committed to growth and training in these arts. The woman's needs were met when she touched the fringe of Jesus' garment and Jesus affirmed their relationship, saw her awesome courage and giftedness, and allowed his priorities to be shaped by the encounter.

And so Jesus walked on to visit the home of the girl who was dying. "Jesus came to the leader's house and saw the flute players and the crowd making a commotion" (Matthew 9:23).

Flute players were hired along with professional mourners at the time of someone's death. As head of the household and also leader of the synagogue, the father would have been the one in charge of hiring them. There were several mourners, so we know that the father was a rich man as well as a leader. But don't you wonder why the father would have hired professional mourners if he ran to get Jesus and had faith that Jesus would make his daughter well? The father had no funeral plans, and I believe he did not hire them.

Heidi Neumark, Lutheran pastor and author, believes the mourners were "ambulance chasers" looking for business at the funeral. They were like too many of today's religious and political leaders who don't care about people but just want their money and/or their votes—what they can take from others. These professional hypocrites mocked and laughed at Jesus when he said that the girl was not dead, only sleeping. The father was taking a risk by putting his faith in Jesus. Not only would he have had to pay these extra mourners if Jesus failed to heal his daughter, but he would have lost face before the congregation that had elected him. But this father trusted Jesus and followed him into the room of death and agony where his daughter lay. Pastor Neumark puts it starkly: "The father risked his power, his position, his own wallet, and took a gamble on resurrection."[4]

What would that look like today, in the face of the decline of mainline churches? For bishops, pastors, and rostered lay leaders, what would it mean to risk power, position, and our wallets and take a gamble on resurrection? Can congregations and their leaders do the same? Tomorrow and the day after, will you, like the father in this story, continue to gamble everything on Jesus and resurrection?

"But when the crowd had been put outside, he went in and took her by the hand, and the girl got up" (Matthew 9:25). Jesus took the dead girl by the hand. He touched her. In the way of Jesus, you can't love people without touching them, their lives, their issues, their joys and sorrows. The girl was the child of a rich person. The woman who touched Jesus was poor, an outcast. But their stories connect them to Jesus and to each other, just as in the church people of every class, race, and circumstance are equal at the foot of the cross. Here all are welcome. All are loved. All come for resurrection. We can only rise up as one church together.

Death makes us all the same. I learned that painfully on September 11, 2001, in New York City as the Twin Towers fell. "You are dust, and to dust you shall return," God said (Genesis 3:19). Jesus united the woman and the girl, the poor and the rich at the ground zero of death.

We, too, are united. We, too, touch the fringe of Jesus' garment every time we gather as the church, hear God's Word, praise God in our worship, share the Eucharist. Then we go from the chancel to the narthex, and then we move forward onto Resurrection Street.

Go in Peace. See the Poor.

6. A congregation in mission risks new things.

One of the primary insights of the missional church movement is that God is already active in the world, and the church's mission is to join what God is already doing: reconciling and restoring the world. The story of Peter's vision in Acts 10 can help us understand our mission.

Peter was staying at the home of a tanner named Simon in the city of Joppa during the early days of the church, after the dramatic events of Pentecost. He went up on the roof to pray while he was waiting for lunch, and while he was praying, he went into a trance.

But the story does not start with Peter. It begins with God working in a Gentile named Cornelius. Up the coast in Caesarea, Cornelius, a Roman general, was also hungry. He was seeking God. He sent for Peter, whose fame as a spiritual leader was growing rapidly. Would Peter, a Jew, come to see this Gentile spiritual seeker? Cornelius wanted to know if the God of Peter and Abraham and Sarah and Isaac also loved Gentiles.

Back in Joppa, Peter, in his trance, saw all kinds of animals descend on a tablecloth. He was hungry, but the food was not kosher. He would dishonor God by killing and eating what was ritually unclean. But then he heard God say, "Get up, Peter; kill and eat." When Peter protested, God said, "What God has made clean, you must not call profane" (Acts 10:13-15). This happened three times, and then the tablecloth was lifted and Peter came out of his trance.

The men sent by Cornelius then appeared at Simon's gate and asked for Peter, and God told Peter to go down and meet them. They told Peter they wanted him to come with them and teach them about the true God. The next day, Peter left with them.

In the living room of the Gentile Cornelius in Caesarea a few days later, Peter declared, "God shows no partiality, but . . . anyone who fears him and does what is right is acceptable to him" (Acts 10:34-35).

This remarkable story of God's grace crossing boundaries turns on the trance of Peter the daydreamer on Simon's roof. The English word *trance* is inadequate, suggesting a kind of woozy reverie. The Greek word for "trance" is *ekstasis*, a dynamic word from which we get the word *ecstasy*. *Ekstasis* means literally "to step forth." It is an "out of the box" word. It is the shift in consciousness of Peter, hungry on a rooftop, who in a moment of *ekstasis* was made vulnerable to the imagery of the tablecloth full of animals, unclean as well as clean. The insight about God's inclusion of the Gentiles, which had been repressed and resisted by his everyday consciousness and worldview, overwhelmed him in the state of openness and receptivity that is *ekstasis*. For Luke, the gospel writer and the writer of Acts, ecstasy is the business of the Holy Spirit. *enthused*

Many congregations are involved in mission strategy discernment these days, encouraged by their local and national denominations. But no program or process will get us anywhere if we ourselves aren't moved to ecstasy by the urgency of the Good Shepherd seeking the lost sheep. Mission begins with the hunger for ecstasy, for the kind of experience that is open to the urgent interior word of the living Christ who dwells in each of us. Life in Christ asks us *to step out* continually into wider worlds, deeper spiritual insights, passionate engagement with the calling we have from God.

What do you see when you look out the window or down from the roof? Consider these lines from the poem "Mirrors" by Nikki Giovanni:

> Windows show who we hope to be
> Mirrors reflect who we are
> Mirrors . . . like religious fervors . . . are private.
> And actually uninteresting to those not involved
> Windows open up . . . bring a fresh view.
> Windows make us vulnerable.[5]

Ecstasy means leaving the usual behind. After listening to God on the roof and then listening to the men sent by Cornelius, Peter had a choice. He could go to Cornelius, or he could stay where he was.

Several years ago, I had the opportunity to join David deFreese, then bishop of the Nebraska Synod, in visiting several inner-city Omaha congregations. We walked the streets, met with leaders, listened to the story of each congregation and its neighborhood. The next morning, all of us met together in the bishop's office, and I shared a few observations, which we discussed together. One pastor, longing to connect with his community, pointed out three schools within eyesight of the congregation he serves. His church is located on a hill overlooking a challenged community. I asked him if he had ever had a one-on-one conversation with the principals of the schools. He hadn't. A year later, I came back to see how things were going. The pastor couldn't wait to see me. He had gone down the hill and listened to each principal, then teachers, then parents. Now the congregation was being renewed by rerooting in its community via the schools. His ecstasy was palpable. Community gardens, after-school programs, and many more new tables testified to the power of the Holy Spirit to move us from ecstasy to action.

7. A congregation in mission makes all decisions based on its mission.

After baptizing the Gentile Cornelius and his household, Peter had some explaining to do in Jerusalem.

> "And as I began to speak, the Holy Spirit fell upon them just as it had upon us at the beginning. And I remembered the word of the Lord, how he had said, 'John baptized with water, but you will be baptized with the Holy Spirit.' If then God gave them the same gift that he gave us when we believed in the Lord Jesus Christ, who was I that I could hinder God?" When they heard this, they were silenced. And they praised God, saying, "Then God has given even to the Gentiles the repentance that leads to life." (Acts 11:15-18)

Peter's report to the church at Jerusalem was a watershed experience in the history of the church's mission. After the Romans destroyed the temple in Jerusalem in 70 CE, some believers despaired, wondering whether God's promises had failed. However, as Lutheran theologian David L. Tiede has pointed out, two forms of Israel's faith survived and dispersed in the empire. The Pharisaic school, which had been forged in the synagogues following the first destruction of the temple (587 BCE), became the rabbinic Judaism of the second century. The followers of Messiah Jesus became the Christian movement, predominantly Gentile by the mid-second century. Both traditions embodied the scriptures. To illustrate why Peter initially met with uneasiness among the leaders in Jerusalem over the baptizing of Cornelius and his household (Acts 11:3), Tiede quoted from the rabbinic Mishnah (a collection of Jewish traditions compiled in the second century CE): "Moses received the Law from Sinai and handed it down to Joshua, and Joshua to the elders and the elders to the prophets, and the prophets handed it down to the men of the Great Assembly. They said three things: Be deliberate in judgment, raise up many disciples, and make a fence around the Torah."[6]

This enclave strategy preserved Jewish communities for centuries. "Be deliberate in judgment." The community had to be preserved and protected from ecstasy. "Raise up many disciples." Israel's enclave faith was more a matter of teaching and learning than acting and telling and reaching out. "Make a fence around the Torah." Israel's faith and practice had to be pure and protected from contamination. If all Israel were to keep Torah for one day, Messiah would come. Israel was God's enclave of holiness on earth.

The book of Acts shares the story of how the messianic message of faith in the crucified and risen Lord burst this enclave. The apostles of Jesus fanned out to the network of synagogues throughout Asia Minor, Greece, North Africa, and the Roman Empire. The good news could not stay inside the synagogues. Its reach had been described in a great commission delivered by the prophet Isaiah:

> "It is too light a thing that you should be my servant to raise up the tribes of Jacob and to restore the survivors of Israel [restoration is good, but not enough!]; I will give you as a light to the nations, that my salvation may reach to the end of the earth." (Isaiah 49:6)

Luke and Acts tell the story of how God turned Israel outside of preserving itself into an instrument of God's saving light for the nations of the world.

The decision made in Jerusalem (Acts 11:1-18) set the course for Christian mission. Think of the beautiful formula for the church from the

Nicene Creed: one, holy, catholic, and apostolic. Each element is a facet of the diamond through which the church's beauty is illumined. If the council in Jerusalem had begun with "one" or "holy," Peter would have required Cornelius to observe the Law and become circumcised before taking a place at the table. But the council began with "apostolic," that the church is sent in mission. Peter gave his testimony to the inclusion of Cornelius and the Gentiles at the table. That decision trumped every other decision that could be made. "When they heard this, they were silenced. And they praised God, saying, 'Then God has given even to the Gentiles the repentance that leads to life'" (Acts 11:18). In the future, every important decision was mission-driven. When apostolic mission sets the table, other priorities fall into place or fall away.

What drives the decisions of congregations, synods, and communions? Enclave survival? Or the mission of being "a light to the nations"? We must ask of every budget line item, every choice we make:

- How will this train and strengthen our missional leaders?
- How will this help us listen and act in the community?
- How will this help us strengthen the faith and discipleship of every member?
- How will this help us join God active in the world?
- How will this help us build and renew tables of relationships of reconciliation and restoration for the life of the world?

8. A congregation in mission is clear about money and relationships.

"They gave themselves first to the Lord and, by the will of God, to us" (2 Corinthians 8:5). That simple sentence written by the apostle Paul, depicting the offering of the Macedonian Christians, gets to the heart of what is at stake in the mission support and stewardship of the church and each of its disciples. Money, mission support, and the offering of the Macedonian Christians are a referendum on relationships. Priorities are clarified: this is a spiritual issue.

By examining 2 Corinthians 8:1-15 more closely, we can see that this is a text for a time such as ours. Paul is in conflict with the church in Corinth. In fact, relations had soured between Paul and the Corinthian church after his first letter to them. He was accused of being too bold in his letters but too weak in person. Things had deteriorated to the point where Paul decided to cancel a planned visit (so as not to stoke the controversy) and to send a letter instead. In 2 Corinthians 2 Paul refers to this letter as one "with many tears" (v. 4; it was probably sent between the writing of 1 and 2 Corinthians).

Painful visits. Letters with tears. Conflict. A lousy economy and the suffering poor. Does this sound at all similar to our time? Congregations that are experiencing declining membership and resources, including money, can become anxious. This anxiety can lead to conflict. We begin to think that God is holding out on us, and we become anxious about our very survival.

And at a time like this, when the church in Corinth was in conflict and the churches in Jerusalem and Macedonia were experiencing extreme poverty and suffering, at exactly this auspicious time, Paul decided to take an offering! Yet in the midst of conflict and fear, it is always God's time. The time is now.

> Now concerning the collection for the saints: you should follow the directions I gave to the churches of Galatia. On the first day of every week, each of you is to put aside and save whatever extra you earn, so that collections need not be taken when I come. And when I arrive, I will send any whom you approve with letters to take your gift to Jerusalem. (1 Corinthians 16:1-3)

Seeing clearly the context of Paul's appeal, its spiritual framework, is very important. The congregation is fighting, in conflict. Paul is not shy about that. But they are still ambassadors. They still have the ministry of reconciliation entrusted to them. The resurrection has changed everything. And, likewise, because of our renewed relationships through forgiveness and repentance, we rejoice. Our mutual patience and endurance in Christ give us complete confidence in one another by the grace of God. Paul has confidence in the Corinthians. God has confidence in us. God's confidence becomes our own. Spiritually confident leaders pay attention to the connection between money and relationships.

And these relationships are solidified in our relationship with God, who joins us together and provides the resources for the mission table. In

2 Corinthians 8, notice that when Paul describes the situation of the Macedonian Christians, he begins with the grace of God. The grace of God is the only reason we talk about stewardship. The Greek word for grace, *charis*, is used four times in this text. The Macedonians' opportunity to give and their willingness to give are described as *charis*, grace. What God has done and what God continues to do in and through us sets the mission table.

Consider the juxtaposition: the Macedonians' abundant joy and extreme poverty (2 Corinthians 8:1-2). God seems to be saying something to us here. The poorer the people, the more generous they are. Or maybe the most reconciled, the most generous. During a terrible famine in Africa, Transfiguration Lutheran Church in the South Bronx, like the Macedonians, a congregation of and for the poor, gave more to the ELCA World Hunger Appeal than any other congregation in the same synod. If you have been on a mission trip, you have seen that in the places of the deepest poverty, the people almost stumble over themselves to give a lavish welcome. At a welcome banquet, the humble and joyful hosts share poetry, prayer, and songs and dances composed for the occasion.

Extreme poverty . . . abundant joy. And notice these words and phrases from the text: "wealth of generosity," "voluntarily," "beyond their means," "privilege of sharing." Joy and grace jump off the page. These descriptors paint a contour of the life of a disciple and the shape of mission. And there's accountability here. You made a beginning; complete the work. Do what you said you would do. This stewardship takes in all of us. By that I mean everything that we are—in faith, in speech, in knowledge, in eagerness, in love.

After praising the Macedonians, Paul gets to motivating the Corinthians in 8:8. Paul says blatantly that this is not a command. But he is wielding an iron fist of accountability in a velvet glove of grace, reconciliation, and the joy of renewed relationship. Actually, Paul is commanding the Corinthians by pointing to Jesus Christ. First the Macedonians gave themselves to God. In a similar way, Paul commands the Corinthians by pointing to the example of Jesus Christ, who, though he was rich, yet became poor for our sakes. So Jesus Christ embodies abundant joy and extreme poverty, a wealth of generosity, voluntary giving, and the privilege of sharing. It is an imitation of Christ that is evoked in this offering. Be accountable to that!

In verse 13 we learn about ancient economics. The far-flung churches involved in this offering are geographically diverse and also diverse in terms of wealth and poverty. Paul is saying that the way in which we share our wealth captures how we see our relationships. It's a new kind of economics that mirrors Acts 2:42, where the new church shared what they had as they were tending to prayers, meals, and the teaching of the apostles. Each, as he or she was able, gave so that none was in want among them. German theologian Ernst Troeltsch called this the "religious communism of love."[7] There is something about relationships that is critical here in how Paul, and Jesus, understood how money works.

Paul was invoking the patronage system in Greek and Roman culture. In that context and culture, giving money bestowed power, status, and honor. Giving charitably or patronizing the arts built power for the giver. As Paul said, some give because they can, and some receive because they must. That is a heartless equation, so Paul begins with the gifts of the poor, not the neediness of the poor. And Paul begins with seeking to protect the collection by stressing equality and reciprocity.

This is really an image of an interdependent church. And, of course, these relationships are cued right at the beginning of the Macedonian offering. For, first, the Macedonians gave themselves to the Lord. They did that by repenting after they fought with each other. And then, by the will of God—God wants this—they gave themselves to the church. Our stewardship rests on relationships, both individual, one-to-one relationships and communal relationships, being interdependent and living for others.

In the way of Jesus, the power ladder is inverted. The last shall be first, and the first shall be last. That is the spirit of the Macedonian offering. A transformed patronage system speaks to the church's radical call to relationship and inclusion with and among the poor.

Here is why stewardship and mission support are so important for a congregation in mission. We live in a time when we can no longer count on institutional loyalty. People fund and support things that move them. Fund-raising and other means of resource development will continue to be important. The offering envelope alone does not cut it anymore. And that is fine. A church in mission participates in the economy of its context.

But at the heart are these relationships. Mission begins with each disciple, every day, transformed by gratitude for the gift of new life through the death and resurrection of Jesus. It begins with a gracious God and our response.

Paul's second letter to the Corinthians invites us to see ourselves as Macedonians. And as Macedonians to see ourselves as part of the whole church. We are in this together. God's mission has a church. In other words, at exactly that point where a spirit of conflict or fear or scarcity is the most powerful—when we look for what reduction in spending will help us survive given the economy and all the other pressures—the gift we make to the wider church becomes the Macedonian offering. By the will of God, they gave themselves to us.

9. A congregation in mission is propelled by the resurrection of Jesus.

When visiting our son in the Peace Corps in Ukraine where he was teaching, we met a wonderful woman named Nina. She was a fellow teacher, and her husband had been an officer in the Soviet Army. Things were tough economically for everyone at the time. "It's our reality," she would shrug as she spoke of long bread lines, high unemployment, electricity blackouts, and rising crime.

Nina had been raised on Soviet atheism and taught to be cynical of any sign of religious faith. She knew I was a pastor. She had sized me up and apparently decided I seemed like a regular guy, not a religious fanatic or someone who would fall for irrational answers to deep questions. Nina was an atheist. Nina was spiritually hungry. One day she looked at me and simply said: "Really, I mean really. Do you really believe all this religious stuff? That there is a God? Really! What do you believe? Do you really think there is more after death? I mean, really!"

Well, that is the question, isn't it?

We in the church will not truly give ourselves to God's mission in the world until we are stunned once again by the resurrection of Jesus from the dead. Our call to mission, like Paul's, comes from the risen and living Christ. Being a church that gives our hands to God's work is not merely a matter of human organization; it rises from Christ's seizure of those he chooses.

Through the call to mission, the risen Christ wrestles with, humbles, trans-figures, and embraces those whom he chooses to endow and send.

The apostle Paul made clear throughout his ministry that his mission, like ours, was born on Easter. He never got over that resurrection appearance on the road to Damascus:

> "While I was on my way and approaching Damascus, about noon a great light from heaven suddenly shone about me. I fell to the ground and heard a voice saying to me, 'Saul, Saul, why are you persecuting me?' . . . Since I could not see because of the brightness of that light, those who were with me took my hand and led me to Damascus." (Acts 22:6-7, 11)

For Paul, this experience was both conversion and commissioning as an apostle.

In Italian artist Caravaggio's painting of the scene from 1601, Paul is flat on his back with legs outstretched, arms raised up to heaven, and eyes shut since he has been blinded by the resurrection light. The central figure in the painting is the horse, which is shown sensitively lifting its hoof so as not to tread on the poor creature sprawled beneath its belly in the dust. The encounter with the risen Lord is a devastating one; it lays Paul on the ground in absolute vulnerability. Unless that is our church—every baptized person and every congregation as a center for mission and every institution and network in the fabric of our church—lying there in the dust and blinded by the light, we will never recover the Great Commission to "go therefore and make disciples," to baptize and to teach them the way of Jesus Christ (Matthew 28:19-20).

Reclaiming mission is to be again stunned by the resurrection of Jesus from the dead, to reclaim our utter dependence on the risen Lord. Paul knew that to be an apostle was to be utterly dependent on grace, always ready to be broken again by encounter with the truth, to be vulnerable, needy. It means to live where contradiction and controversy cross and clash; it means being opposed as well as loved; it means to be cruelly confronted by grotesque unfaithfulness in the church as well as stunned by wonders of love and creativity. To be a baptized Christian, a synod, a congregation, or a denomination is to be on a road where you will be thrown down into the dust again and again by the risen Christ who has seized hold of you.

In Acts 22, after Paul recounts the story of how he was stunned by the resurrection, he takes his hearers with him to the temple in Jerusalem. He is frightened, clinging to the enclave. His mission is going badly. He faces opposition. The congregation is at risk.

> "While I was praying in the temple, I fell into a trance and saw Jesus saying to me, 'Hurry and get out of Jerusalem quickly.' . . . Then he said to me, 'Go, for I will send you far away to the Gentiles.'" (Acts 22:17-18, 21)

Paul experienced that shift in awareness away from the normal condition of anxiety and preoccupation into an openness in which he became aware of Jesus as dynamic presence and Word.

Jesus burst death's three-day prison. The resurrection of Jesus and the Great Commission bursts the fearful enclaves too many of our congregations and too much of our church business have become. The resurrection of Jesus transforms congregations at risk to congregations risking mission. Every ministry is a ministry "at risk" if it does not share the kinetic ecstasy that leads it to step out into wider worlds. Stunned like Paul by the resurrection of Jesus, we are ready to listen—to God, to partners in the household of faith, to our neighbors in the world, to signs of a resurrection still going on today.

Where mission is a matter of technique, assembly resolutions, the latest program, or a way to preserve the enclave, it ends up in barrenness and frustration. The Great Commission flowing from the resurrection of Jesus depends on prayer. Its real leaders are women and men who experience inner movement, *ekstasis*, away from the defended, anxious state into a place where they see Christ speaking to them, saying, "Go, go, go."

- What do you see when you are in the ecstasy of resurrection trance?
- Whose hand lifts you up from the dust when you are blinded by resurrection light?
- What pulls you forward at the intersection of enclave and mission?

Christ is risen indeed! Stunning!

10. A congregation in mission is shaped by Word and sacraments.

The late Aidan Kavanaugh, a scholar of liturgics, said that the integrity of evangelism—that is, sharing the good news of God's grace—is directly related to the integrity of the liturgy.

The very nature of this Christ-shaped community became its evangelizing power. Acts 2:42-47 describes what was and is, indeed, a new kind of table in the world where everyone is welcome, everyone eats, and everyone shares. In the wake of the Pentecost conversions to life in the risen Christ, those who had been filled with the Holy Spirit set a table in the local households. Assembly around the holy things became the form of mission. The community was drenched in prayer. In this community, everyone had gifts to give and everyone at the table was supported. The teachings of the apostles moored their life together. People grew in their young faith, and as they did, they shared this burgeoning hope with others. The quality of the table they set became known.

Day by day the Lord set a place at the table for new brothers and sisters, kin in Christ. It is a picture of the shape of mission today. Our world is hungry for tables of integrity where there is a place for everyone to make a difference in the world, bring their gifts, and step out into wider worlds and deeper faith. And so for us, mission is the legs we put on our prayers and liturgical practice.

The heartbeat of this Christ-shaped community is Word and sacraments. Consider the mission heartbeat of baptism. We do not baptize our babies (of any age) and leave them at the font. Baptismal ministry follows them into the world: to care and struggle for the schools in which they learn, to guard the communal values that shape them, to nurture their relationships, and to provide them with mentors. A vision of a well-lived life in society is baptismal mission.

Consider this story of Dottie Maria Gonzalez's baptism. John, the president of the congregation I served in New Jersey, was the owner of a factory in Paterson. One day he asked me to meet him there to talk about baptism with one of his employees, an eighteen-year-old father. The expected baby's mother was sixteen. They were immigrants, not members of any parish, and the baby's arrival had rekindled their curiosity about the church and its sacraments. I met them in a corner of the factory, and between my broken Spanish and their broken English, we had a conversation about their baptismal hope for their soon-to-be-born baby. Our weekly sessions of baptismal preparation, instruction in the faith of the church, were attended by many of the other workers during lunch hour.

When their child, Dottie Maria, became a child of God through baptism, the president of the congregation and many of their fellow factory workers stood at the font with the young father and mother and baby. Because of that baptism, the congregation participated in a church-based community organization dedicated to improving the schools of their local communities. They could not leave Dottie Maria at the font. Word and sacrament ministry in a congregation became word and sacrament ministry in a factory, which became mission and ministry in the community.

Consider the mission heartbeat of the Eucharist. If we eat at the altar table of our congregations and others outside do not eat, or eat alone, eucharistic ministry is to follow the real presence of Jesus into the world to connect with the community.

The missional power of the Eucharist became vivid for me after one of many encounters with some of the most vulnerable in our society. His name is Ricky. I pulled into the driveway of a motel, one of North Jersey's refugee camps for the homeless. As I got out of the car, a three-year-old boy came rushing at me, shouting, "Give me the money! Give me the money!" Ricky knew that my clerical collar meant help. My money meant another night of shelter before resuming residence in an abandoned car.

Marie, Ricky's mother, was a young widow. She called the church because it had earned the dubious reputation as the one place someone could go when there was nowhere else to go. Her husband had died in a drug shootout across the bridge in Washington Heights, Manhattan. As I approached room 7, she came out, telling her son to be quiet. He was pitching a fit. Every time I tried to talk, the boy shouted, "Shut up!" until I lifted him up, thrust his little face parallel to mine, and said quietly, "No. You be quiet." Then I sat down with Ricky on my lap.

He was quiet as his mother told me her story, the daily destruction of two human lives. God was setting a table here. Ricky snuggled closer into my arms. After listening for a while, I got up to pay for their room for a couple of nights. I put Ricky down.

"Don't go," he said.

"I gotta go now, sport," I said.

Ricky and his mother were part of a process of mission discernment in which our congregation and others in our conference were engaged. Homeless women and children emerged as a high priority. The integrity of our congregation's table would have something to do with a new table at a welfare hotel by the George Washington Bridge.

After baptizing a homeless child and his mother, the congregation could not resist the missional power of the sacraments. We bought the house next door and began planning transitional housing for homeless women and children. There was much resistance from the community, and some from the congregation itself, but the leadership resolved to see this through. The Sunday before the first mother and her two children began to live in the house next door, we lived into the power of the Eucharist. After the communion liturgy but before the benediction, the entire congregation processed to the house next door. We went from the Lord's Table out into the street. The crucifer, acolytes, book bearer, and children carrying bread and wine from the altar led the family of Jesus into the house next door. We put the bread and wine on the kitchen table. In groups we gathered around the kitchen table. We imagined a mother and her children around the table. In the kitchen, we prayed for the mother and her babies, for this sacred kitchen table, and we gave a prayer of thanks that we were privileged with our new neighbors to be guests of Jesus. We then reassembled in the church for the benediction. "Go in peace; serve the Lord," echoed into our ears as we left for our own kitchen tables to continue living out eucharist.

In an intense, renewed focus on local congregations, we will rediscover the primary missional power of baptism and eucharist for the life of the world.

Seventeen Marks of a Missional Congregation

We have been listening to God through the biblical drama as we seek the contours of our congregations as mission tables. The following list distills some of these insights to help us listen at our congregational tables.

1. *Word.* A missional congregation is a community of the Bible. It offers a variety of opportunities for members and the community to dwell in the Word.

2. *Children.* A missional congregation has the children of church and community at the center of its attention, program, and budget.

3. *Worship.* Excellence in liturgy, preaching, and music anchor the life of a missional church. A missional congregation understands that Word and Sacrament are its heart, its power.

4. *Solidarity.* A missional congregation is joined at the heart with its conference, synod, and churchwide partners. It is linked to ecumenical partners.

5. *Infrastructure and money.* A missional congregation does its business well and relates truthfully and transparently to money issues.

6. *Leadership.* A missional congregation invests in leaders and has a plan for leadership development. The congregation sees everything it does as opportunity for leadership development.

7. *Mercy and justice.* A missional congregation invests in programs and is part of networks that work for both social service (mercy) and social change (justice). A congregation that turns its face and the face of Jesus to the poor, the stranger, and those without the gospel is always being renewed.

8. *Community.* A missional congregation is connected to its community in two ways. First, the life and presence of the community are institutionalized in the congregation through programs in which neighbors walk through the doors every day (early childhood centers, 12-step programs, social ministry programs, the arts, etc.). Second, the congregation is always present and listening and serving outside the doors, in the midst of its community (church-based community organizing and its listening arts are critical to this goal).

9. *Wider worlds.* Mission and discipleship take the church and its members into ever-widening worlds. In its membership, a congregation will reflect its immediate community. In its wider participation in ministry and networks, it will relate to wider worlds (companion synods, church-based community organizations, feeding programs, etc.).

10. *Communal leadership.* Pastoral leadership belongs to the whole community and encourages active participation of the laity.

11. *Story.* A missional congregation can tell its ancestral and founding stories. Every member is able to tell his or her faith story.

12. *Spiritual gifts.* A missional congregation organizes its life at the intersection of the spiritual gifts of its members and the mission of the congregation to its members, its community, and beyond.

13. *Vocation.* A missional congregation releases leaders into the church and community, including rostered leaders, leaders on boards of colleges, leaders in social ministry organizations, and leaders in other church and community organizations.

14. *Stewardship.* An ethos of abundance saturates a missional church with grace and releases generous stewards into the world.

15. *Prayer and the faith.* Prayer and faith practices of the disciple permeate every meeting, decision, and area of congregational life. The ethos of missional discipleship creates the context for parish life.

16. *Action and reflection.* This approach guides the study of scripture, leadership development, and deepening communal and individual discipleship.

17. *Resurrection.* A missional congregation lives in the power of Jesus' resurrection from the dead. In the risen Christ all things are possible.

Read and Reflect, Discuss and Reflect

1. Read Acts 1:6—2:21 and Acts 2:41-47. What do the passages say to you, at this time and place, about God, the church, and the wider world?

2. Review the seventeen marks of a missional congregation above. Where is your congregation strong? Where does it need to grow? What are some other marks of a missional congregation you would add?

3. Review the ten biblical marks of a missional congregation that were discussed in this chapter.

   1. A congregation in mission is always listening.
      - Share an experience of a time when someone's listening showed you great care and love.
      - How does your congregation practice listening in ways that create a space for people to experience Christ's love and care?
   2. A congregation in mission mentors and trains its leaders.
      - Share an experience of being mentored into a new skill or a new role.
      - How does your congregation mentor people of all ages to help them develop a new skill or take on a new role?
   3. A congregation in mission nurtures communal leadership.
      - Who are the worship leaders in your congregation? Do both pastors and laypeople lead worship?
      - How does your congregation share and develop leadership among a variety of people?
   4. A congregation in mission faces paralysis with courage.
      - Was there a time when you were angry with God and had that anger transformed into something healing or life giving? Share your experience.
      - In what ways is your congregation being courageous at this time in its life?
   5. A congregation in mission reroots in its community.
      - Has there been a time in your life when you felt you could only "touch the hem" of Jesus' garment—that is, keep to the

extreme edges of the church, the body of Christ? Where did you find the courage to seek help? Share your experience.

- In what ways is your congregation involved in ministering to people in your community who are afraid to seek help or who feel like the church is not a place for them?

6. A congregation in mission risks new things.

- Have you ever witnessed someone risk power, position, or resources because they believed Jesus' promise, "Those who find their life will lose it, and those who lose their life for my sake will find it" (Matthew 10:39)? What happened as a result of taking the risk?

- What risk could your congregation take in its ministry at this time for the sake of joining God's reconciling and restoring mission in the world?

7. A congregation in mission makes all decisions based on its mission.

- In what ways is your congregation an enclave focused on self-preservation?

- In what ways is your congregation focused on building tables to include people previously excluded from its work and ministry?

8. A congregation in mission is clear about money and relationships.

- Share a time when you were grateful for some way God acted in your life or the life of a loved one.

- How did your gratitude give way to thanksgiving and sharing yourself or your resources with others in some way?

9. A congregation in mission is propelled by the resurrection of Jesus.

- When have you encountered the risen Christ in ways that changed the direction of your life or moved you deeply?

- Has your congregation ever experienced a ministry or program dying and something new being raised in its place?

Can you think of something in your congregation today that might need to die so that God can raise something new?

10. A congregation in mission is shaped by Word and sacraments.

- Share a time when you experienced worship connecting in a concrete way to the wider world.

- What are some ways that your congregation's ministry of Word and sacraments spills over into the lives of your neighbors?

CHAPTER 5

Mission Table Leadership

As he walked by the Sea of Galilee, he saw two brothers, Simon, who is called Peter, and Andrew his brother, casting a net into the sea—for they were fishermen. And he said to them, "Follow me, and I will make you fish for people." Immediately they left their nets and followed him. As he went from there, he saw two other brothers, James son of Zebedee and his brother John, mending their nets, and he called them. Immediately they left the boat and their father, and followed him.

—Matthew 4:18-22

The decline of institutional religion is calling us into ministry in a new context here in North America. Yet the United States remains unique in the world when it comes to spirituality. Eighty percent of the US population is still convinced that God is real. So here is our context: institutional forms of religion are collapsing while most people still believe in God. We are awash in spiritual hunger. In this in-between place, we do not yet know what forms will emerge. All things are possible. In such a time as this, what kind of leadership can come alongside congregations, communities, and spiritual seekers, helping them to imagine new mission tables, revise old ones, and learn from what they see emerging?

Prophets and Priests

The call of leadership today is to be women and men of God. This is a prophetic role, calling people back to their spiritual moorings and their baptismal vocations. We call these the practices of faith: praying, worshiping, studying scripture, and struggling for justice. Missional leaders build tables that are spiritual oases of service and solidarity with the lives of communities in this secular yet believing context.

The only two leaders in the Bible called humble are Jesus and Moses. We are told, "Moses was very humble, more so than anyone else on the face of the earth" (Numbers 12:3). At the burning bush, God was not seeking a weak, self-effacing leader, but someone with enough passion to have fought for an abused slave (Exodus 2:11-12) and with the courage to go to Pharaoh and make a demand. Humble Moses told powerful Pharaoh, in the name of God, "Let my people go!"

Jesus said, "I am gentle and humble in heart" (Matthew 11:29). Humble Jesus defied Roman imperial power for the sake of God's reign and the transformation it sets in motion. Both Jesus and Moses lived in faith and hope that the vision that drove them was God-given.

So what does it mean that the leadership of Moses and Jesus can be described as humble or meek? Maybe this humble leadership orientation has something to do with the beatitude "Blessed are the pure in heart, for they will see God" (Matthew 5:8). Moses was so taken by being in the presence of God on Mount Sinai that his face burned with the glory. Jesus was so filled with the presence of God that he continually called out to his Father with thanksgiving in the midst of his healing and teaching.

The church's mission needs leaders infused with the presence of God, confident in the promises of God, and filled with the hope that comes with being humble before God. In that humility is strength, integrity, resolve, and a single-minded embrace of the possibilities the risen Christ makes present. We need leaders who are spiritual. We need leaders who are vulnerable and yet confident, who understand what the apostle Paul meant when he said, "I am content with weaknesses, insults, hardships, persecutions, and calamities for the sake of Christ; for whenever I am weak, then I am strong" (2 Corinthians 12:10). We need leaders who pray and love scripture and are fearless as they engage the unknown future.

We cannot talk about leadership in the church without talking about the call every Christian receives at baptism to be part of God's mission in the world, to be part of the priesthood of all believers. The church today needs leaders who are committed to agitating and winsomely engaging its members and neighbors around that call.

Baptismal Promises and Practices

Several years ago as Lent approached, the leaders of the congregation I served in New Jersey were wondering where so many of the recently baptized and their families had gone. Our church had been baptizing about twenty people a year. We decided to use Lent as a time to connect again with the baptized. A team from the congregation visited the home of every person and family baptized in the previous ten years and invited those people to a baptismal reunion. They asked them to bring pictures of the baptism and family pictures of their growth. Many of the baptized did come, and new tables emerged.

At the reunion, we went through the baptismal liturgy, especially the promises. We talked about worshiping with children in church. We began a conversation on the nurture of children, which grew into a parenting support group, to which we invited the school, Sunday school, and community. That support group became a port of entry into the life of our parish. Everyone who did not come to the reunion received another personal visit, and we distributed the materials we had shared. The reunion became an annual event. When we began to see baptism not just as an event "'cause granny wants us to get the kid done," but as a lifelong process, we began to understand the missional power of this watery witness. A river runs through it.

The rite of Affirmation of Baptism offers congregations a way to engage all the baptized in the faith practices that undergird the daily vocation of every disciple as well as support mission strategies and the leadership needed to set and renew mission tables.

"You have made public profession of your faith."

The mission of the church is public. Creating nursery schools, latchkey programs, church-based community organizations, and other programs that link the life of the parish to the life of the community is part of the baptismal witness of the whole church. Because our faith is public, the church's mission moves us from the kitchen table to the altar table to new tables in the world.

"Do you intend to continue in the covenant God made with you in holy baptism?"

The key word here is *continue*. Rather than onetime events, marriages, funerals, baptisms, and confirmations are processes of the Holy Spirit's activity, abiding opportunities for the church to stay in touch with people in the Spirit's power.

"Do you intend . . . to live among God's faithful people?"

Living among God's faithful people is called *koinonia* in scripture. It means to participate in or to belong to one another and to Jesus. It is the koinonia of the cup and the loaf embodied in human community where we bear one another's burdens. Koinonia is Lydia's Table in Brooklyn, a ministry with young adults where the liturgy takes place around a table as a meal prepared by the congregation is served. It is support groups and Bible studies in homes in the midst of communities.

"Do you intend . . . to hear the word of God and share in the Lord's supper?"

The heartbeat of the life of the church will always be the Book, the Bath, and the Meal—the Bible, Holy Baptism, and Holy Communion. As neighborhood children in the city are invited, building by building, to Sunday school, Jesus is both the one inviting and the one shared. In one urban neighborhood, homeless men who are parish members take the palms from the Sunday of the Passion liturgy and distribute them to residents of the welfare motels nearby, inviting them to church.

"Do you intend . . . to proclaim the good news of God in Christ through word and deed?"

"Word and deed" anchor the mission statement of Trinity, Lower East Side, New York City. The groundbreaking for their new building was witnessed by hundreds—from the bishop to local street people. The building incarnates in bricks and mortar "In Word and Deed." On one floor is a soup kitchen and shelter. Another houses the sanctuary for worship and Christian education. Another provides space for a parsonage for the pastor's family. A river runs through the baptismal vision of Trinity.

"Do you intend . . . to serve all people, following the example of Jesus, and to strive for justice and peace in all the earth?"

The biblical word for service is *diakonia*. Our example, Deacon Jesus, Servant Jesus, thought equality with God not something to be grasped but emptied himself and became obedient, even to giving his life on the cross (Philippians 2:6-8). Service is the primary gift for carrying out the church's mission and for every baptized person's vocation. In addition to its local congregations, the church's social ministry organizations, disaster response and immigration ministries, and global ministries of service undergird Christ's presence in all things.

Nine Characteristics of a Mission Leader

With this baptismal grounding of leadership and its connection to the "priesthood of all believers" in the world, let's take a look at some basic characteristics of a mission leader. These characteristics are meant to paint a picture of what both clergy and lay leadership might look like for today's context. The insights of seminary deans and seminary students are incorporated into this list, which will become even stronger as we continue to reflect and learn together across the church how the Holy Spirit is endowing today's leaders.

1. A mission leader is relational.
2. A mission leader pays attention to institutional relationships and networks of support.
3. A mission leader has an entrepreneurial spirit.
4. A mission leader is clear about the power of money.
5. A mission leader builds a strong cadre of local leadership.
6. A mission leader is a witness to the presence of the risen Jesus.

7. A mission leader roots deeply in the community.
8. A mission leader is adaptive.
9. A mission leader is a servant leader.

1. A mission leader is relational.

Does she like people? Will he put in the time and energy needed to build relationships within the congregation and in the community at large for the sake of the reign of God? Relationships are the synapses of mission.

The account of the disciples on the road to Emmaus in Luke 24:13-35 illustrates the relational rhythms of leadership. Two people are on a journey. They share the news, their grief, the things on their hearts. Jesus joins them on the way. Such journeys of the spirit are the heartbeat of setting mission tables. Note the rhythm of listening and relationship building and the spiritual depth of this encounter.

> While they were talking and discussing, Jesus himself came near and went with them. (Luke 24:14)

This story places the activity of Jesus and the church out in the world. Jesus fell in step with the disciples. He entered their world.

> And he said to them, "What are you discussing with each other while you walk along?" (Luke 24:17)

Jesus listened to these followers' concerns and drew them out. The encounter was about them at that point in their journey. A mission leader is always helping people listen to one another about the times of their lives and equipping them as listeners for spiritual seekers in the world who touch their lives.

> But their eyes were kept from recognizing him. (Luke 24:16)

These disciples were grieving. The world around them was spinning, and they were too. When we come together at the table, we must be open to encountering one another in new ways. We think we know one another, but we do not. I am not the same person I was three months ago, and neither are you. We are always changing, growing, becoming. We always have a need to encounter one another again and again.

> Then one of them, whose name was Cleopas, answered [Jesus], "Are you the only stranger in Jerusalem who does not know the things that have taken place there in these days?" He asked them, "What things?" (Luke 24:18-19)

The two most important words in the text are "What things?" These forlorn disciples did not recognize Jesus. With those two words, he drew them out, asking about *their* experiences and showing a commitment to place the conversation *where they were at* on the road. He didn't initially shout, "Hey, this is me!" Instead, he fell in step with them. He listened and connected with the real stuff of their journey.

> Then he said to them, "Oh, how foolish you are, and how slow of heart to believe all that the prophets have declared! Was it not necessary that the Messiah should suffer these things and then enter into his glory?" (Luke 24:25-26)

Only after hearing their lament did Jesus draw them to himself, the living Christ. Truthful, loving feedback is an important part of any deepening relationship. At the right time, a mission leader knows that we can help each other interpret our journeys in the light of the gospel's promises.

> Then beginning with Moses and all the prophets, he interpreted to them the things about himself in all the scriptures. (Luke 24:27)

The living Christ meets us in the Word. The Word comes alive when we answer Jesus' question "What things?" What things have taken place in our life journeys? A mission leader connects the Word to our journeys on the road. The biblical story centers and animates our listening and relationships at the congregation table and in the conversations that flow from that table into the world.

> But they urged him strongly, saying, "Stay with us, because it is almost evening and the day is now nearly over." So he went in to stay with them. (Luke 24:29)

Our listening and tending to relationships come out of the hospitality of the table. Mission leaders invite Jesus to "stay with us." The mission of the church is the network of these invitations to Jesus to join us on the road and stay with us as we journey.

> When he was at the table with them, he took bread, blessed and broke it, and gave it to them. Then their eyes were opened, and they recognized him. (Luke 24:30)

The listening and the relationships flow to and from the table of the Eucharist. At the table, we literally become companions with "those with whom we share our bread," with Jesus and one another. Mission leaders recognize that Jesus' presence at the heart of our relationships renews the mission that emanates from the congregation table.

> That same hour they got up and returned to Jerusalem; and they found the eleven and their companions gathered together. (Luke 24:33)

The Emmaus disciples lived and believed beyond their own kitchen table. They were part of the larger company of disciples, just as our congregations are linked to wider and deeper relationships and mission in the body of Christ in the world. They returned to Jerusalem to share what they had learned. They were accountable to the body of Christ and the overall mission of the church. A mission leader makes these broader connections and values the mutual accountability.

> Then they told what had happened on the road, and how he had been made known to them in the breaking of the bread. (Luke 24:35)

After their encounter on the road with Jesus, the disciples became witnesses to his resurrection. A mission leader helps each disciple to grow in the ability to share his or her faith story.

As I reflect on my parish ministry, I realize that mentoring relationships were always forming. For more than a year in one congregation I served, I never knew that the sexton was a musician and a poet. William Garcia, a quiet and competent high school kid, cleaned the church on Sundays. A year into our polite relationship, we finally had a real conversation as part of a series of one-on-ones I was doing in the congregation. Our church was contemplating beginning a liturgy in Spanish, and so I was meeting with and listening to some of our bilingual members. William and I sat for over an hour in the church basement. I listened as he told me about his passion for the violin, his love of poetry, the jumble of his chaotic family life, and his efforts to hammer out an education and musical excellence from the local schools. Looming over our conversation, as it does for most city kids, was the street. I asked, "Will you meet with me an hour a week for a month and teach me about your world? Oh, and by the way, will you play your violin in church sometime?" He smiled.

William and the other Hispanic members became my mentors in mission, setting a new table. When we began our liturgy in the Spanish language, it was William who accompanied the hymns on his violin and who wrote the prayers of the church in language of poetic beauty. He played, prayed, and led because one day I stopped ignoring him and listened.

2. A mission leader pays attention to institutional relationships and networks of support.

- Does the leader help the congregational table connect to other tables? This is especially important for those who develop new congregations and other new ministries.
- Does she show up at gatherings where other leaders are present?
- Does he regularly have one-on-one conversations with his bishop and other synod leaders for mission?
- Is she preaching and leading Bible study for local congregations supporting the mission?
- Is he a steward of the wider mission of the synod and denomination, helping those around his table to understand what they are a part of and that we can do together what we can never do alone?
- Are the stories of unfolding ministry being shared?
- Is she surrounding herself with a "kitchen cabinet" of strong mentors and supporters?

Studies of new mission starts have shown that where local networks and relationships are strong, *and connected to the wider church*, so is the fledgling ministry. It takes a village of tables to nourish and raise a new one. The Council of Jerusalem launched Paul to build a new mission table with the Gentiles. He remained accountable to it and nourished by its prayers, leaders, and resources. Mission leaders today must not be lone rangers.

3. A mission leader has an entrepreneurial spirit.

- Is she casting a compelling vision and adjusting it to the insights of a growing network of supporters and leadership?
- Does he build momentum with incremental victories as the ministry is being built?

As a bishop, I loved attending the anniversary celebrations of congregations and hearing their birthing stories of entrepreneurial courage. Members spoke wistfully of sweeping away the beer cans and debris of Saturday night at the VFW hall and setting the chairs on Sunday morning for the liturgy. People remembered canvassing door to door in their communities, inviting children to the first Sunday school. In the past, planting churches has generated a restless excitement. Our communal memory of excitement and bold risks for mission will be a path to the renewal of our beloved tables for the life of the world.

4. A mission leader is clear about the power of money.

- Is her sense of stewardship deep and communicated?
- Is he building a strong, long-term financial model to sustain the ministry?
- Is the money lined up with vision, and is the mission leader courageous in asking for sacrificial support?

As we considered in chapter 4 regarding the Macedonian offering, a mission leader affirms the congregation as an integral part of the whole diverse church and of God's mission.

5. A mission leader builds a strong cadre of local leadership.

- Is she always in leadership development posture?
- Is leadership development part of budget decisions about the best possible ongoing training for leaders?

- Does the leader practice action-reflection in mentoring others?
- Is the development of local leadership the highest priority and the way to evaluate and measure mission effectiveness?

I learned the priority of building strong local leadership from the community organizers who touched the life of my parish ministry. Each year I would think of four or five leaders with whom I would spend some time. We would do a series of one-on-one meetings, and at some point I would bring them together. We would study scripture, pray together, and think communally about our congregation and its mission. Together we would identify four or five potential new leaders we wanted to nurture. Over the years, the circle grew, as did the arenas in which burgeoning leadership could be trained, mentored, and agitated for spiritual maturity.

It began with Barbara. She was the most effective chair of an evangelism committee I have ever met. Under her leadership we began many programs for neighborhood children, an outreach in the Spanish and Korean languages, and systematic visitation of Sunday school and nursery school families. We became involved in church-based community organizing. Barbara was full of ideas, a creative leader with many contacts in the community. And she began her leadership because of a one-on-one encounter we had. Before she became a leader, she was a semi-active member who worshiped occasionally. But she was grateful for what the congregation had done for her when her mother was ill and how her children were accompanied by the parish when she went through her divorce. Her ability and willingness to tell her story with gratitude and deep conviction suggested to me that we had an evangelist on our hands. The transitions in her life suggested that she was at a growing point in her journey of faith. We met for five one-on-one meetings to talk about her spiritual life and the possibility of church leadership. During that time, we shared our spiritual journeys, dreamed together about the mission of our congregation, prayed for each other, and then reached a covenant about her willingness to lead and the support I would give her.

6. A mission leader is a witness to the presence of the risen Jesus.

- Can she tell her faith story and encourage and teach others to tell theirs?
- Does he ground mission in scripture and prayer?

One year we were seeking fresh ways to have the stewardship conversation in our congregation. After church I asked some of the leaders, those with evident spiritual maturity, to join me in the basement for lunch and conversation. I asked one question: "When has this church been there for you when you needed it?" A couple of hours later, through stories that brought tears of gratitude and recognition, we had the beginnings of our stewardship journey. The ability to tell the stories of our experience at the table of our congregation became the means to root our hearts, minds, and wallets around gratitude for the presence of the risen Christ in the passages of our lives through our seats at the parish table. The leaders took turns telling their stories as the sermon each Sunday, which evoked the stories of all of us gathered at the table.

7. A mission leader roots deeply in the community.

- Is she engaging the community in a regular discipline of one-on-one relational meetings?
- Is the "hem of the garment" of the mission placed where the community can touch it?

  > Then suddenly a woman who had been suffering from hemorrhages for twelve years came up behind [Jesus] and touched the fringe of his cloak, for she said to herself, "If I only touch his cloak, I will be made well. Jesus turned, and seeing her he said, "Take heart, daughter; your faith has made you well." And instantly the woman was made well. (Matthew 9:20-22)

- Does he understand the public missional power of baptism and eucharist?

As discussed in chapter 4 and the story of Jesus healing the woman with a flow of blood, a mission leader notices people who "touch the hem" of Christ alive in the life of the church.

8. A mission leader is adaptive.

In the church today, a leader must know how to come alongside people and institutions, helping them discern their spiritual lives and vocations and their roles in a wider ministry. This collaboration requires multicultural competence. A mission leader embodies accompaniment, a leadership characteristic closely allied with an entrepreneurial spirit.

This type of leadership is "adaptive" as opposed to "technical." *Technical leadership* uses tried-and-true solutions to recognizable problems and challenges. There is a program, an approach that can move things forward. In contrast, Ronald Heifetz, founding director of the Center for Public Leadership at Harvard's Kennedy School of Government, describes what it meant for one group to exercise adaptive leadership: "They had to go beyond what people expected of them, risk testing some relationships, and move themselves and their organizations into unfamiliar territory. . . . They each learned in the midst of action, made some mistakes and mid-course corrections, and stayed the course."[8] *Adaptive leadership* accepts that we are in a new situation, that we don't have technical means to move forward, that we are willing to risk and learn and probe the future. Adaptive leadership is collaborative. It means engaging the future together, risking together, making mistakes together, and learning together.

For congregations, this means setting new tables and mission probes and seeing where they take us. It means the willingness to invest in promising probes and to learn from those that do not gain traction. We will try and fail with the understanding that we do not know the exact shape of the future, only in whose hands the future lies.

Adaptive leadership is all about listening to God, to our congregation, and to our community and the relationships and tables emerging from what we hear. The apostle Paul left the synagogue and went outside the walls of the city of Philippi to encounter economic migrants from Thyatira (Lydia and her friends and family) and to see where the encounter would take them (Acts 16:11-15). A congregation conducting hundreds of one-on-one conversations with undocumented workers living in their neighbor-hood—at Laundromats, bodegas, and street corners—and having over one hundred show up at its first Spanish liturgy on Easter Sunday is practicing adaptive leadership.

9. A mission leader is a servant leader.

In the way of Jesus, through the perspective of the cross, leadership is given to us in the most unlikely places in powerful ways.

When we invite all God's children to the table, sometimes to our surprise they show up. Edgar was a strange character who lived alone in a welfare motel when he wasn't homeless on the street. He often walked two miles to our church. He was a bit rough around the edges. On occasion he could get loud and demanding, and so my heart sank on Palm Sunday when he was waiting in the sanctuary for me after a full day of liturgies, first communions, and pastoral conversations in the sacristy and narthex. I knew that when Edgar appeared, he wanted a ride, some of my time, some bits and pieces of what I could produce toward his survival.

I wanted to go home. On the drive back to his motel, he talked my ear off and criticized the sermon, and I prayed for patience. Yet something strange and wonderful began to occur as I pulled into the parking lot of the run-down Motor Inn. A door opened, and an elderly woman emerged. She knocked on another door, and another elderly woman peeked out. They limped to our car. Others waiting at the edges of the parking lot followed.

They were expecting us. I was in someone else's church now. For the first time, I noticed that Edgar's hand grasped a bunch of palms. He had promised to bring them palms from our liturgy, and one woman was already standing at the car door waiting for hers.

Here's the thing: when victorious Abram showed up in King's Valley to represent God before the king of Sodom, Melchizedek showed up with bread and wine (Genesis 14). There were already priests of God on the ground. God will make a way to procure leaders to bless the people.

Edgar, with all his rough edges, was the only person who had ever passed for a pastor in that backwater parish of broken souls. I tell you, there could be no more fertile soil for biblical "church growth" than this concrete parking lot and its waiting children of God and their wisdom "from below."

Edgar gave the woman a palm branch through his window. She clutched her piece of palm as if it were an exquisite diamond. I could only watch in awe as the palms from our liturgy were distributed among those hungering for Jesus in the shadow of the George Washington Bridge.

Edgar got out of the car. "Bless us!" he commanded me. I got out of the car, blessed their palms, placed my hands on each forehead, and pronounced a benediction. If I had had bread and wine, I would have fed them right there. Palms from one table to another. The Passion of Jesus flowing from the altar to tables of the vulnerable, where Jesus was already waiting.

This is the displacement of the church for which God is preparing leaders and a universal priesthood.

Read and Reflect, Discuss and Reflect

1. Read Luke 24:13-35. What does the passage say to you, at this time and place, about God, the church, and the wider world?
2. As you experience life in the church today, what are things that effective leaders do?
3. In what ways have leaders in the church helped you develop your gifts to share with the church and the world?
4. The nine characteristics of a missional leader discussed in this chapter are not an exhaustive list. What is on your list?
5. You can use the flow of the Emmaus road story as a framework for small group and mentoring conversations:

   - "Show and Tell." Meeting on the road, sharing something of our journey during the week, including its current issues and growing edges, and asking, "What things?"
   - "Into the Word." Making connection between the biblical drama and our journeys—"He interpreted . . . the things about himself in all the scriptures."
   - "The Growing Edge." Insights into spiritual gifts, growth in faith and vocation—Were not our hearts burning within us . . . ?"
   - "Making Connections." Opportunities in the church and world for ongoing service and growth—"Their eyes were opened, and they recognized him."
   - "Mutual Propositions." Being accountable to one another and to the mission of the church in concrete "next steps" in the walk of faith—"They got up and returned to Jerusalem."

CHAPTER 6

Setting Mission Tables

Now the wife of a member of the company of prophets cried to Elisha, "Your servant my husband is dead; and you know that your servant feared the LORD, but a creditor has come to take my two children as slaves." Elisha said to her, "What shall I do for you? Tell me, what do you have in the house?" She answered, "Your servant has nothing in the house, except a jar of oil." He said, "Go outside, borrow vessels from all your neighbors, empty vessels and not just a few. Then go in, and shut the door behind you and your children, and start pouring into all these vessels; when each is full, set it aside." So she left him and shut the door behind her and her children; they kept bringing vessels to her, and she kept pouring. When the vessels were full, she said to her son, "Bring me another vessel." But he said to her, "There are no more." Then the oil stopped flowing. She came and told the man of God, and he said, "Go sell the oil and pay your debts, and you and your children can live on the rest."

—2 Kings 4:1-7

On a cold February night some years ago, I experienced a rite of passage in my understanding of mission. Two thousand followers of Jesus created a table in the midst of creation. They met with the mayor of

New York City to negotiate issues like crime, drugs, and affordable housing as they struggled to reroot the life and mission of their congregations in their communities. These issues came out of listening within congregations and with their neighbors and ecumenical allies.

Out of such efforts to set tables in the public arena, thousands of affordable housing units were built in the burned-out section of Brownsville, Brooklyn. Kitchen tables set in barren, broken streets. This affordable housing became known as Nehemiah Housing, from the Old Testament book of Nehemiah, which tells of the rebuilding of the walls of Jerusalem. This grassroots effort of Christians from various communions to literally rebuild their part of the city with new housing accessible to poor and middle-class folks in the midst of creation is a sign of the new, emerging solidarity in Christ that will "name" and "bless" the world as communion with God. These houses not only shelter but also dignify life from God. I learned that the path to *renewal of a congregation* is directly connected to the *renewal of its community.*

Thousands of congregations throughout the country work for community renewal through interfaith and broad-based groups that are affiliated with organizing networks. For me connecting with these networks has been life-giving and game-changing. Many of the insights and perspectives in this book, in fact, are embedded in the arts of faith-based community organizing. I encountered community organizers from the Industrial Areas Foundation (IAF) early in my ministry in Queens. The stance of listening in the community and the resolve to do "one-on-ones" regularly, within both the congregation and the community, come directly from the training and consultation I received from organizers like Greg Pierce, Dick Harmon (now involved with the Leaven Project in Portland), Michael Gecan, David Nelson (with Nehemiah Housing in Brooklyn), and others.[9]

As we explored in chapter 5, leadership for ministries rerooted in their communities requires us to revisit and reclaim the priesthood of all believers. Who is included in "all"? Mission embraces everyone at the table, not just pastors or rostered leaders. Let this leadership find its natural place in service in solidarity with our neighbors. In *diakonia* ministries of grassroots mobilization, service, advocacy, and new and renewed congregations of the church, the poor, strangers, and those who do not know the story of the cross and resurrection of Jesus are not objects of charity or a result of neglect of broken tables, but sacraments of the hidden presence of Jesus, cocreators of restored reconciling tables.

The 2 Kings 4:1-17 account of the prophet Elisha and the widow with a jar of oil gives us a framework for the possibilities of throwing our lot in with one another in setting tables for rerooting in the community. It begins with a grieving wife at her wit's end. She cries out in agony (and, I think, anger) at Elisha: "Your servant my husband is dead; and you know that your servant feared the LORD, but a creditor has come to take my two children as slaves" (v. 1). She is at the bottom. Think of your congregation, of life together in a mainline Protestant denomination in a time of the shrinking church. In such an aging church, the creditor who is taking away our children is the society in which our children no longer hear the songs of our mothers and grandfathers. When we lose catechesis, that effort to pass the faith from generation to generation, we lose those generations to the life of the church table. So, too, the widow is without a future.

Elisha's question is interesting. "What shall I do for you?" (v. 2). The woman is not completely powerless. She can still name what she needs. She has agency. We need leaders who can come alongside widowed congregations, seemingly bereft of a future, and agitate their agency. What do you need? What do you want? Invitation to mission strategy can become the turning away from aimless, powerless drift. It is the question that Jesus asked the paralytic, stuck in apathy and anger on his mat in John 5: "Do you want to be made well?" (v. 6). Elisha's question is God's question to all of us. "What do you want from me?"

The next question digs even deeper. Elisha is getting the widow to see that she isn't powerless. "Tell me, what do you have in the house?" (v. 2). Indeed, what do we have in the house? The widow thinks she has nothing. Life's cupboard is bare. That is how we sometimes act in our churches—afraid of the future, as if we have nothing, as if God is holding out on us. "Your servant has nothing in the house, *except a jar of oil*" (v. 2, emphasis added).

So, what do we have in the house? What's in your house? Listening in the church begins with this question. What does your jar of oil look like? Is there some wine in the house? Bread? Water? Faithful leaders? Rock-solid values and convictions? Songs of grandparents? The Book? A table? Stories of when the church was there for you when you needed it? Moments of grace and forgiveness? Prayers when you need them and a casserole at the door when you come home from the hospital? A cross?

What, indeed, do we have in the house?

Then Elisha turns into a good community organizer. He tells the woman to leave the house and engage her neighbors in the community. Ask what is on their tables, in their houses. "Go outside, borrow vessels from all your neighbors, empty vessels and not just a few" (v. 3). The hardest thing in the world to do when we are depressed, grieving, dulled into damning routine is to leave the house and seek our neighbors and ask for their help. Elisha is telling us through the widow to reconnect with God's community. Conferences and synods and denominations and ecumenical allies still matter, even if their vessels seem empty. When we leave the kitchen and altar tables and move to the tables of our communities and wider world, God has empty vessels waiting for our oil, company for our grief, mutual signs of hope, the ransom of our children, the collective pouring out of our future.

When a congregation begins the journey of mission discernment together, it will begin to reroot its life in the ebb and flow of the life of its wider community. It claims what it has in the house, a gathering of the empty vessels of its neighbors, always listening to God and believing that God will work a miracle with their gifted solidarity. It is about being stunned by the resurrection of Jesus. The widow just kept pouring into the empty vessels until God provided, through her oil and her neighbors' vessels, a renewal of her hope, the liberation of her children and her future.

The Three Great Listenings

Early in my parish ministry, I learned about the effectiveness of community organizing in helping congregations become competent in their mission of setting tables in new public spaces as signs of God's new creation. Central to the art of community organizing is training leaders in how to listen.

At the heart of setting tables for mission are "the three great listenings"—listening to God, listening within our congregation and among our allies in other communities of faith, and listening outside the doors of our congregation to our neighbors in our communities. Mission discernment comes about from listening in these communities.

1. *We listen to God* explicitly in prayer, study of scripture, and liturgy; we witness to the presence of God in our lives and the world around us. The narrative of the death and resurrection of Jesus for the life of the world shapes us and the tables we set.

2. *We listen to the church.* God's mission has a church. We listen for the gifts and assets God has given us in our congregation. We listen to our denominational partners and our ecumenical allies, to the many ministries, networks, institutions, and agencies to whom we are joined in mission. We set broad, gifted tables for mission. The whole church participates in God's mission.

3. *We listen to the world around us.* We are continually doing one-on-ones with our neighbors, listening to their hopes, aspirations, insights, and giftedness. We train the disciples in our congregations to do this kind of listening. We listen to public leaders, to police and school officials, and to business leaders. We study demographics and trends; we reroot church tables in the tables of our communities.

In the three great listenings, we listen to the Holy Spirit as we imagine what our grace-based presence will be like in the public life of our neighborhoods tomorrow and ten and twenty years from now. How will the Spirit guide us as we "listen" into existence new and repaired tables in our churches and communities for the life of the world?

Anatomy of a Mission Table

Here is how one such effort, anchored in renewed local relationships, helped to plant a South Asian mission in New York City. Around the year

2000, the ELCA Northeast Queens Conference engaged in a synodical *Re-rooting in the Community* (this is the name we used for our Area Ministry Strategy process). Most of its congregations were struggling; some were very near closing. The neighborhoods of the conference were filled with new immigrants. (Flushing, New York, has the largest Korean community in the United States.) This rerooting process is similar to many in use throughout the ELCA and its ecumenical partners. The congregations, Lutheran schools, social ministry organizations, and other Lutheran and ecumenical institutions join together in a discipline of prayer and discernment, study of scripture, listening, training, and relationship building as they plan for mission.

These building blocks of the process used in the Northeast Queens Conference are central to any approach that is effective and faithful:

- Listening to God.

  ▷ The initial training sessions lifted up the centrality of Word and sacraments and presented stories from the biblical drama that illuminate listening, mentoring, building community, developing leaders, and fulfilling public mission. (Many of these Bible stories are included in chapters 4 and 5 of this book.) The ELCA Book of Faith Initiative, which seeks to reconnect the church with the Bible, permeates the process in use today.

  ▷ The participants in these sessions covenanted to join together in the process.

- Listening to each other in the church and to those in the community.

  ▷ Training in conducting one-on-one interviews and small group "house meetings" led to a disciplined listening presence in both the congregations and their communities. Living testimony was shared by members and neighbors, grassroots ownership of proposals was developed, real issues were identified and addressed, and the church was exposed to potential new leaders.

  ▷ Strategic "dream teams" of five to ten people were formed for the conference, and each congregation and ministry partner analyzed the interviews and collected demographic and statistical data in order to identify issues and implications for mission.

▷ Several conference consultations were held in which member congregations wrestled with these issues and their implications as mutual support and solidarity in mission emerged.

▷ The conference and each ministry partner drafted a mission statement.

▷ Concrete proposals for the mission of the conference and each ministry partner were developed.

▷ Throughout the process, training sessions were held in evangelism, leadership development, and mission centered in Word and sacraments. Participants gathered for worship, prayer, and Bible study to keep the process focused on Christ.

▷ Participants received training and gained experience in multicultural competence as well as in how to overcome resistance to change and how to build momentum for engagement and impact.

Listening in the community provided testimony to the demographic evidence that a burgeoning South Asian community would respond to outreach that joined spiritual needs to childcare and child development issues, to learning English, and to other immigrant needs. Demographic information was given flesh-and-blood human tapestry through hundreds of one-on-one conversations with neighbors. It was the local mission team of the conference that set the table for this ministry.

ELCA churchwide partners, the pastor of the first ELCA South Asian mission in Chicago, and synodical leaders came to the table. The key here is that national and global resources were convened at the local Area Ministry Strategy table in Queens. Durable, sustaining partnerships were formed for funding, launching, and sustaining the mission.

St. Paul Lutheran Church in Floral Park, Queens, was chosen as the best site for a South Asian mission. It was struggling for survival, it had a great facility, and its leadership was ready because, in the rerooting process, they had renewed their relationships to the other conference congregations and the synod leadership. A local conference mission team coordinated the process.

Global mission tables connected with local mission tables. Pastor Daniel Peter, from the Andra Pradesh Lutheran Church in India, was doing a similar outreach to South Asians in Hong Kong through global mission partnerships. He accepted the call to begin the South Asian ministry in Queens. The local mission team and the synod mission director welcomed Pastor Peter and his family, built an apartment in St. Paul's large facility, and walked with them as the ministry began. The ministry was named Ashirwad ("divine blessing" in Sanskrit). Its mission and programs matured into a growing congregation in close relationship with the English-speaking members of St. Paul's. The neighborhood outreach, with ecumenical and interfaith support, became a critical outreach into the immigrant community beyond South Asians. The conference congregations joined to form a conference youth ministry. Pastor Peter brought renewal of evangelical zeal and helped lead door-to-door outreach in the neighborhoods of other congregations in the conference.

Finally, the growing congregation, while not losing its South Asian focus, organized as St. Paul International Lutheran Church, and today it serves people from around the world.

That was the experience of the Northeast Queens Conference. In a process such as this, the church's future can be secured by turning itself toward the larger community, toward its human need and those without the church in their lives. A cadre of missional leaders emerges. The process becomes a platform where tough institutional decisions can be made about the future viability of individual congregations in renewed relationships. And collective action can be brought to emerging mission opportunities.

Tables emerge and converge as empty vessels fill with overflowing oil.

Tables for Community Engagement

Such Area Ministry Strategies are happening across the country, from East Portland, Oregon, to Omaha to Detroit. From the prairies to the suburbs to our inner cities and exurbs, new tables for ministry strategies are being set. These new tables are renewing relationships at the grass roots, helping congregations and their allies reroot in their communities as they find paths to their futures.

Children's Memorial Lutheran Church in Kansas City serves the poorest of the poor. But it has gone through much internal change and struggle, and its viability as a sustainable institution has been in question. Over the years, it has been heavily subsidized by synodical and national resources, and the money shared with the ministry has added up to a large amount. Partnership support from synod and churchwide funds has largely kept the ministry afloat, and annual conversations have usually addressed how much support would continue to be poured into the ministry.

New leadership and the end of a long period of conflict seemed to offer hope for a different conversation. As the congregation approached funding partners for another round of subsidy, they agreed to ask a new question. Rather than "What can the funding partners do to continue to sustain Children's Memorial?" they asked, "What is the vision for mission in the Kansas City metropolis in which Children's Memorial is embedded?" In a meeting with the bishop, the synod's director for evangelical mission, and key leaders in the Kansas City area, a willingness to engage the three great listenings emerged. Out of this discernment process, proposals for a strategy for mission and ministry in the area transpired.

After floodwaters ravaged Minot, North Dakota, and put four of its congregations underwater, the ELCA looked at Minot as a new mission field, and national resources—Lutheran Disaster Response, congregational renewal, and economic development—joined forces for the first time. Partners in the effort were pastors and leaders of Minot area congregations, Lutheran Social Services, the local campus ministry, and others. They studied scripture and prayed together. They listened to one another's laments, hopes, and dreams. They talked about what the three great listenings might look like in Minot and went back to their congregation councils to discuss participation in this process. Partners prayed for one another in their discernment. One by one the leaders came back with favorable recommendations. As the bishop checked off each "yes," I saw people numb with grief begin to recover some of their agency and hope.

Community consists of those who throw their lot in with each other and who know who the others are. These partners had listened to God and to each other, and the next day at a hotel downtown they began listening in the community. The local bishop led three meetings. Over breakfast, leaders of each of the congregations met with public officials, from the mayor to people in the senator's office. Midmorning they met with non-profit leaders. At lunch they met with business leaders. They asked two questions in each meeting: "What are the main issues emerging from the flood?" and "What is your vision for the future?" Issues began to emerge, and a new table was set amid the heartbreak of Minot.

Why Building an Area Mission Table Matters

During the height of the Roman Empire, when their boats reached the shore of Britain, it is said that the Romans dragged their boats ashore and burned them on the beach. The message was blunt and clear: We are here to stay. A congregation expending its resources, imagination, and leadership to reconnect to its community and to set a new mission table needs to have a "burning our boats at the shore" commitment.

For twenty-five years, the ELCA has been a church body in which only 3 percent of its membership is nonwhite with a primary language other than English. Despite our best efforts, that 3 percent number has been persistent and implacable. And it will not change until we Lutherans "burn our boats on the shore." Until mission priorities and strategies become local, until we together plant and renew the church where the people live, we will have only the comfort of our convictions and be an overwhelmingly white enclave of Northern European heritage in this increasingly globalized country.

The majority of our communities live with no contact with the life of the church. The "nones" (a term for survey respondents who claim no religious affiliation) dwarf the numbers of churchgoers. To burn our boats on the new shore of this emerging multicultural and religiously disaffected America is to invest in congregations that are connected to their communities. We need both new Word and Sacrament communities of faith and older congregations reconnecting to their communities. It is at the local font and altar where strategies for spiritual, relevant engagement with our changing communities are transformed into flesh-and-blood tables of hospitality, care, and renewal.

New congregations are not thriving, according to a 2012 study. They are not moving from outside support to sustainable local support.[10] Too many of these ministries are, in fact, dying, closing, or barely hanging on. And these are added to the growing numbers of existing congregations reaching the limit of their viability and sustainability.

What's that all about? Many things, but surely this: the church is out of relationship at the grassroots level where it lives. Congregations watch new ministries planted in their midst struggle and sometimes close, yet they do nothing. In the way of Jesus, no congregation ought to struggle and die alone. We are not connected to one another in real, missional struggle as we should be. Too often congregations have also lost their connection to their communities and the everyday struggles and issues of their neighbors, including immigrants. Mission initiative needs to return to the grass roots of the church in renewed relationships among local congregations (Lutheran and ecumenical partners) and in rerooting the lives of our congregations and institutions of the church in their communities.

It is time to reconnect, to leave our individual congregation tables and set new tables where we are asking each other, "What might we do together that we are unlikely or unable to do on our own?" Out of these mission discernment tables, we will be enriched by renewed relationships that will accompany our new starts as well as struggling and dying congregations. Multiple new and renewed tables will be forged.

All mission is local—from the kitchen table to the altar table to ever-widening tables for the life of the world. What would it look like for every conference, cluster, or local ministerium to be a platform for evolving mission strategies that come from listening to communities, from asking, "Who's missing?" and then together seizing the future? What would it look like for new congregations—and for renewed missional congregations—to have local partners and support right at the time of birth?

What if these local conference strategies were formed by collective faith practices? When the local community and congregations are engaged in corporate mission planning, communal spiritual practices such as worship, prayer, the study of scripture, discernment, stewardship, and advocacy take on an urgency and spiritual depth that renew both church and community.

The only hope for clunky, dying institutional structures is for denominations to reroot their empty vessels as close to the ground as possible. The ELCA is calling and sending a director for evangelical mission to each synod to sit at the table and work with the staff of the local missionary bishop in order that the vast resources and institutional strength of the larger church can accompany emerging local tables for new and renewed congregations. We are organizing an apostolate to and with our communities and the wider world.

Our collective attempt to be partners with and artisans of human community does not in itself bring in God's reign. Rather, the multiracial, ecumenical efforts of God's people to participate in the unfolding of their piece of God's creation, to set new tables there, can be seen as signs of sacramental living. Undergirding this mission moment are two bottom-line convictions: that as in the beginning, God does not act unilaterally in creation but through the tables God sets through us; and that as human beings, we are not autonomous but nested, entwined in relationships at tables for the life of the world.

Read and Reflect, Discuss and Reflect

1. Read 2 Kings 4:1-7; 1 Corinthians 12; and 1 Peter 2:9-10. What do the passages say to you, at this time and place, about God, the church, and the wider world?
2. When have the gifts of your community surprised you? What assumptions about your congregation's neighbors and community might be obstacles to your setting a mission table together?
3. Using the image of a glass half full, half empty (think of the widow's oil jar), if the community in which your congregation is located is a

glass half full, what resources and gifts does it contain? What about your congregation?

4. Review the three great listenings described in this chapter. List the ways in which your congregation currently

- listens to God.
- listens to the church, both the congregation itself and the wider faith community.
- listens to your community and the world around you.

What is one new way or opportunity for your congregation to

- listen to God?
- listen to the church, both the congregation itself and the wider faith community?
- listen to your community and the world around you?

How soon can you begin the three great listenings in your congregation?

- See the Model for Congregation Listening Tables below.

5. Think of a time when you or your congregation made a commitment or investment akin to the Romans "burning their boats on the shore." What was difficult about that total commitment? What were the rewards? What were the surprises? What did you learn that might aid in setting your congregation's mission table?

Model for Congregation Listening Tables

1. Maximize participation and gather input from as many people as possible.

    - Make the listening tables short-term and highly focused. Small groups of six to ten people meeting for 45 minutes are recommended.
    - Schedule listening tables during gatherings that are part of regular parish life—choir rehearsals, Bible classes, confirmation classes, Sunday coffee hours, and church council and committee meetings.
    - Be sure to contact those who do not attend one of the listening tables.

2. Establish clear ground rules.

    - Meetings will begin and end on time.
    - Groups will consider four questions, spending up to ten minutes on each question.
    - Each person in a group will be invited to respond. After that, the group can discuss the question if time allows.

3. Recruit three leaders for each listening table.

    - *The host* has a ministry of hospitality: welcoming participants, preparing refreshments, and making sure that people are introduced to one another.
    - *The convener* runs the meeting, opens with prayer, explains the ground rules, keeps track of time, and ends the meeting with a prayer or blessing.
    - *The scribe* listens carefully and takes meeting notes. (After the meeting all three leaders go over the notes, adding their impressions and insights.)

4. Train the hosts, conveners, and scribes to listen for three things.

    - *Issues:* Listen for specific issues, not problems. Problems are distant, seemingly impossible to address because they are so pervasive (things like "the declining church," "poverty and hunger in the world," "unemployment," "war and violence," "conflict in the church"). Issues are specific and you can act on them. Rather than "the declining church," there are parents of Sunday school children or visitors who don't come back. Rather than "poverty and hunger" there is the food bank on 9th Street or relevant items in the state or local budget. Rather than "unemployment," listen for particular jobs programs or workplaces.

- *Talent*: Notice the leadership potential in the group. Some participants will be articulate, others will support good ideas, and still others will have wise insights.
- *Passion*: Notice what stirs deep feelings, concerns, and joys within the group. Someone who speaks passionately about her children may be willing to support a youth ministry program. Someone concerned about his mother's ability to live on her own after a hospitalization may want to bring that concern to the social ministry of the parish.

5. Gather people around the listening tables to respond to these four questions:
    - When has this congregation been here for you when you needed it?
    - Name something in your life that is on your heart right now. What gets you up in the morning or keeps you up at night?
    - Name something in the community that is on your heart right now. What issue in the community gets you up in the morning or keeps you up at night?
    - Imagine that our church has received a huge inheritance. Money is no object, there are no restraints. What is your bright idea for what our congregation could be doing in the next five, ten years?

6. Follow up and bring together new tables.
    - Ask each leadership team (host, convener, and scribe) to put together a brief summary of the assets of the congregation (from responses to the first question), issues, and bright ideas that they heard.
    - Bring together members of the congregation to hear and discuss results from this first round of listening tables.
    - Create new tables with people whose ideas and concerns relate to specific issues and opportunities.
    - Create new tables in the community and with allies and partners of the congregation.
    - Provide plenty of opportunities for Bible study and prayer during this time of mission discernment.

CHAPTER 7

Restoring the Broken Table

Then Jesus told them a parable about their need to pray always and not to lose heart. He said, "In a certain city there was a judge who neither feared God nor had respect for people. In that city there was a widow who kept coming to him and saying, 'Grant me justice against my opponent.' For a while he refused; but later he said to himself, 'Though I have no fear of God and no respect for anyone, yet because this widow keeps bothering me, I will grant her justice, so that she may not wear me out by continually coming.'" And the Lord said, "Listen to what the unjust judge says. And will not God grant justice to his chosen ones who cry to him day and night? Will he delay long in helping them? I tell you, he will quickly grant justice to them. And yet, when the Son of Man comes, will he find faith on earth?"

—Luke 18:1-8

The January 15, 2006, issue of *New York Times Magazine* featured people who received a so-called living wage of $9.50 per hour. And yet in 2013 the US minimum wage is $7.25 per hour, with the highest state minimum wage at $9.19 per hour (Washington). Some workers making minimum wage probably feel lucky to have jobs of any kind, but too often they fall beneath the radar, off on the margins, discounted and despised by others. Is it any wonder that Dr. Martin Luther King Jr.'s slogan in the face of dehumanizing poverty of the Memphis sanitation workers in 1968 was this simple: "I am a man"?

Those who struggle to get through each day are people. They are our brothers and sisters:

- disaster victims living in crummy hotels across the country.
- old people who die because they cannot afford medicine.
- millions of people without health care in the US.
- economic migrants despised and sometimes beat up as they toil in this country for just enough for another day.
- children who show up in schools that don't show up for them (during the past several years, hundreds of children in Chicago have been killed).
- children who are abused to death in homes where no one checks to see how they are doing.

The ugly face of poverty, racism, and oppression divides us. The chasm is wide in society when the word of the Lord is rare. More and more of the so-called middle class are losing their homes or are a payment away from losing them. Television news magazines show us schoolchildren living in cars and shelters. Church-related public policy advocates can tell you what that looks like in federal and state budgets and legislation. We don't see the needs of our brothers and sisters when gospel values do not make it to public life.

The table is broken: around the corner, across our country, throughout the world. In what way can our kitchen, altar, and mission tables have any impact at all in living out this promise from Isaiah 58:12: "You shall be called the repairer of the breach, the restorer of streets to live in"?

The Feisty Widow

The cross of Jesus Christ looms over all our tables. It is true that Jesus said, "If any want to become my followers, let them deny themselves and take up their cross daily and follow me" (Luke 9:23). But not once did Jesus say to anyone who came to him for healing, "Your ailment is just a cross you are going to have to bear." Not once did he imply that disability or poverty was simply our lot in life or a punishment for our sins or for those of our ancestors. Nowhere has he suggested to those who struggle with poverty or oppression that they accept their condition or accommodate themselves to the injustice of the world. In fact, they are the very people and conditions through which God has promised to accompany this world as a sign of restoring the broken table.

In Luke 18:1-8 Jesus tells "a parable about [the] need to pray always and not to lose heart." This story illustrates Jesus' preference for outrageous action and the assertion of dignity, pride, and holy impatience: an annoying widow pesters an unjust judge until he gives her what she wants. A literal translation of the Greek has the judge saying, "I will grant her justice so that she will stop battering me." And the punch line is "When the Son of Man comes, will he find faith on earth?" What sort of faith is Jesus talking about?

- Faith like that of this widow, who kept on battering the judge until she got what she wanted.
- Faith like that of the Syrophoenician woman, who wouldn't take no for an answer, who challenged Jesus' dismissal of her with the chilling words "Even the dogs eat the crumbs that fall from their masters' table" (Matthew 15:27).
- Faith like that of Bartimaeus, who wouldn't be silenced by Jesus' impatient disciples (Mark 10:46-52).
- Faith like that of the friends of the paralytic who tore the roof off the house to carry him in so that he would be able to walk out (Mark 2:1-12).

Time and time again, Jesus praised strong, outrageous action from people on the margins of life.

As we practice the three great listenings, the one place that we struggle to listen is at this point of injustice and holy impatience that helps create a demand for change. Nineteenth-century abolitionist Frederick Douglass said, "Power concedes nothing without a demand. It never did and it never will."[11] It is in that sense that I want to talk about the public impact of our mission tables.

Public Tables

We have seen too many ways that religion shows up in the public arena only around issues of private morality, seeking public clout for a variety of issues. These issues often divide "red state" and "blue state" church members and citizens. But how do we leave the defended space of morality battles and find one another at the point of the widow's cry for justice? The God of the Bible is unequivocal about the poor, the stranger, the last, the least, the most vulnerable. Does God's mission have a church in those places?

The church has public tables, rich ways of encountering the most vulnerable in the world, but those tables are often not connected to each other for impact at the point of impatience and demand for change. The "Public Church Engagement" diagram on page 107 presents a continuum of ways the church engages the public, accompanying society with the gospel.

- There are *individual acts of love and mercy*, our serving. Over 90 percent of ELCA congregations are involved in a food ministry of some kind: from putting a can of food on the altar for the Thanksgiving food drive to volunteering in a food pantry or soup kitchen. It is the biblical "cup of cold water," an individual act to alleviate hunger.
- There are *direct services* provided to people in need—social work case management, nursing home care, disaster response, disability ministries, immigration and refugee services, hospitals, foster care of children, legal services, and more. Lutheran Services in America, Lutheran Immigration and Refugee Service, and Lutheran Disaster Response are institutional expressions of this public table.
- There is *economic development* in poverty-stricken communities and their congregations, work such as creation of affordable housing, job development, and sustainable congregational social ministry.
- There is the ministry and faith practice of *advocacy*, which is speaking truth to power by state, national, and global leaders guided by

the public commitments of the church. It is speaking on behalf of the most vulnerable, including people in poverty, the elderly, the disabled, children, the unemployed, and undocumented economic migrants. The ELCA has fourteen state public policy advocacy offices as well as advocates in Washington DC and at the United Nations. They put flesh on the social statements and commitments for justice and equity of the church.

- There is *grassroots mobilization*, community organizing, which is committed to people at the local level having their own power, their own voice, speaking for themselves. It is the angry widow banging on the judge's door.

These public tables are too often not connected to one another. They can become isolated worlds with their own internal conversations and approaches to the public good. Setting mission tables in our communities holds possibilities for linking these tables. Local food banks or direct services

Public Church Engagement

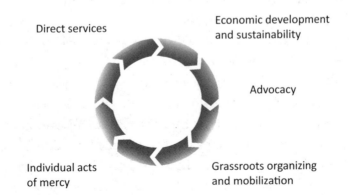

Direct services

Economic development and sustainability

Advocacy

Individual acts of mercy

Grassroots organizing and mobilization

Public Platform Continuum:
Accompanying Civil Society with the Gospel

among people in poverty are places where the church encounters directly the results of inequity in our society. Can those be entry points into deeper advocacy or grassroots community organizing? And how can we link congregational and area mission tables and strategies with these public tables?

People want to show up and make a difference in the lives of people and communities, especially those most vulnerable and suffering. How can the church accompany civil society with the gospel?

Let us get back to the widow in the story from Luke. She is wholly without power. A woman alone in a male-ordered culture, she has few rights of her own. In the Hebrew scriptures, the widow, along with the orphan and the sojourner, are singled out as categories of people who deserve particular care within the community of faith and the wider community. That is because the system was stacked against them. The most likely cause for the woman's suit before the judge would have been the rights to her husband's estate, for it was not uncommon for unscrupulous executors to leave widows with nothing. It is not an exaggeration to say that this case may well have been an issue of life and death for her.

For the judge, on the other hand, it is just another routine matter. Though a person of status and power, he is just another cog in the system that is designed to maintain the privileges of those like him. His role is to dismiss the woman's complaint and strike a deal with her adversary. She might make a bit of a fuss but not enough to make a difference. The deal would be cut, and she would be flicked away like a mosquito to return to her bereft circumstances.

Yet the widow does not play her passive part in the circle of injustice. Unable to compete in the deal to which she has no access, she takes her case public. In a culture in which she has no voice, she refuses to stay silent. She badgers the judge, who complains that the little old widow is beating him up! The widow does not attack the judge's motives or values or credibility. She just wants him to do the right thing! She badgers and batters him until he finally gives in. When he gives in, it is not because he is taking the high road, not because she is right or he has been converted by the force of her argument or is worried about being right with God. He gives in because he has had it with her and wants her to go away.

Theologian Fred Craddock says about this parable of the unjust judge: "In a large gathering of persons concerned about certain unfair and oppressive conditions in our society, an elderly African American minister read this parable and gave a one-sentence interpretation: 'Until you have stood for years knocking at a locked door, your knuckles bleeding, you do not really know what prayer is.'"[12] Jesus commends such persistence—prayer that keeps pounding away until the reign of God comes.

Persistence and Public Exposure

In the arsenal of tools available to public ministry that accompanies civil society, persistence and public exposure are powerful in creating demand for change. This was one of the most important lessons I learned in community organizing. Ideas and spiritual values matter, but they are not enough. Being on the side of those oppressed by poverty and injustice is not enough. If you are not willing to fight, to be tenacious, you will quickly find that Frederick Douglass was right on target: power concedes nothing without a demand; it never has and it never will.

I once heard former president Jimmy Carter say that we live in a world where a person of privilege and a person in poverty never have to interact. We live parallel lives at separate tables. He said that building a house for Habitat for Humanity is mostly an excuse to set a table, to have conversation and interaction between people in poverty and people of privilege. It is about reconciling relationships and building new public space together.

And it is about the public tables of the church's mission where people are listening together. When we truly listen, we communicate three things:

1. *The other is worth hearing.* Listening is an act of recognition. When my mother died, the retired pastor of my parents' church began a weekly visit with my father. They would listen together to a piece of music, and then they would talk about many things and pray together. The weekly visits were life giving for my father. He, his grief, and the road to healing mattered to someone.

2. *The listener values the act of listening.* Listening to another is a ministry of noticing. Noticing lies at the heart of service. The gospels are full of accounts of Jesus noticing people and listening to them.

3. *Our identity as a faith community is always evolving.* When we listen, we learn and readjust to evolving wisdom. When we ask the question Jesus asked on the road to Emmaus—"What things?"—we are in the ebb and flow of our evolving individual and communal lives. When we as congregations and the church cease listening, we atrophy.

Listening meets people at the point of their story, strength, giftedness, passions, insights, dignity, anger, wisdom, and hope.

Presbyterian pastor Jeffrey Krehbiel, playing off the phrase "finding our inner child," suggests that perhaps we need to find our "inner widow." To adopt the faith of the tenacious woman in Jesus' parable is to push ourselves beyond our comfort zones, to take risky action, to discover gifts we did not know we, or those to whom we listen, had, to move beyond social barriers and stereotypes. Jesus' listeners understood full well how poor widows were expected to behave, and the widow whom Jesus imagines is clearly having none of it. She is an older, single woman, alone in the world, with nothing to call her own in a culture that would have made her entirely dependent on the resources of others. Yet she refuses to play the role that society has assigned her. She stands up for herself and does not back down.

The Voice That Keeps Calling

We need to know that our tables are linked across time, connected across the generations. Like telling ancestor or immigration stories around the kitchen table, we need to share such stories together among the various tables of the church. Our day is not the first time tables seem to be so broken, that the church seems to be so challenged, that civil society lives in such conflict. As we seek to set tables in mission today, two ancestor stories can speak to us: the story of Samuel and Eli from 1 Samuel 3:1-20 and the story of Martin Luther King Jr., leader of the US civil rights movement in the 1960s.

In 1967 Dr. King wrote about what it looks like "when the word of the LORD [is] rare . . . visions [are] not widespread" (1 Samuel 3:1): "It is necessary to understand that Black Power is a cry of disappointment. The Black Power slogan did not spring full grown from the head of some philosophical Zeus. It was born from the wounds of despair and disappointment. It is a cry of daily hurt and persistent pain."[13]

I caught a glimpse of some of the reasons for that despair and disappointment when trying to be a spectator in my hometown of Chicago at an open housing march led by King in the 1960s and seeing the hatred on Cermak Road in Cicero. The sheer malice of the crowd screaming out at people marching for decent homes scared me.

Today people who claim to follow Jesus and live by the guidance of Holy Scripture allow ourselves to be divided over private morality while millions in our country and the world barely survive the scandal of poverty and hunger. Dr. King wrote, "The curse of poverty has no justification in our age. It is socially as cruel and blind as the practice of cannibalism at the dawn of civilization, when men ate each other because they had not yet learned to take food from the soil. . . . The time has come for us to civilize ourselves by the total, direct, and immediate abolition of poverty."[14] The God of the Bible is clear about this. Mission with integrity will find ways to stand with the poor and will be a catalyst to help unite the entire church in attending to the poor and the stranger among us, in ending hunger, in moving toward God's dream of equity and justice.

In the time when the Bible tells us that the word of the Lord was rare, a little boy was a light sleeper. He heard a voice calling his name: "Samuel, Samuel . . ." Sleepy and nearly blind, the elderly priest Eli felt the boy's presence at his bed and heard him say, "Here I am, for you called me." Three times Samuel heard his name called, and three times Eli sent him back to bed. Was Samuel dreaming?

The word of the Lord was rare in those days. People didn't frequently have visions. After a period of spiritual depth in the time of the judges, Israel now wanted to be ruled by kings with political power just like all the nations around them. The people were poor and oppressed by their leaders, but the malaise was not primarily economic; it was spiritual. The public table was broken. And Eli's sons, with their greed and hypocrisy, had made a joke of the spiritual life of the land and corrupted even the sacrifices of worship.

Eli would soon realize that the voice calling was the Lord's. And God was not calling him. He would understand that his day was over, his leadership was waning, his time was past. How would he respond when the boy got up again, haunted by the voice calling to him in the night?

And let's open this biblical window even wider. Two things seem critical in a time when the word of the Lord is rare and visions are infrequent. First, Eli and Samuel are *resting by the Ark*, the spiritual table God had set that united the kitchen tables of Israel.

The Ark of the Covenant moved with Israel in their wandering exile, a tangible sign of God's presence. In the Ark was the Torah, God's Word, and it was something like the altar table in our churches today. In times when God appeared to have withdrawn and grown silent in the face of the people's idolatry, when the spiritual leadership of the people was bankrupt, Samuel and Eli were close by the Ark.

The Ark signified the presence of the God who led the people out of slavery into freedom. Dr. King's "Letter from a Birmingham Jail" was testimony from within the shadow of the Ark. It was from the pulpits, churches, and synagogues that the energy and vision for the civil rights movement propelled people who grasped for vision when there had been none. A new public table for civil rights emerged from those who stayed close to the Ark, the altar table. Those tables joined the tables in the public arena with gospel power for justice.

In our time of denominational decline when the word of God seems rare, gathering at our tables—our kitchen tables, our altar tables, our neighbors' tables, our public mission tables—is how we stay close to the Ark. Tend to the Word and Sacrament core of our life together in Christ. Live from the stories of our ancestors—those in the Bible and those passed from one generation to the next. Keep the hope alive. In season and out, rest near the Ark.

A second critical factor in the story from 1 Samuel is that *God keeps calling*. God's pursuit of justice, God's dream of the perfect table in creation, is a restless, relentless vision. Before Samuel's dream and Martin's dream is God's dream. The first words of God's dream were "Let there be." In the beginning, God set a table. God dreamed this beautiful world. God dreamed you and me. It is a dream of abundance in which every human is called to bless all creation by acknowledging the Creator, by partaking of it as life from God. The life between the man and the woman, the end of loneliness, was also part of God's dream. Our life together was meant to be communion with the Creator. Life was sacramental, with every moment, every morsel of food, every surprise of beauty leading directly to the Creator. And God's dream was perverted. We have sold our birthright of abundance for the emptiness known as scarcity. Slavery may be the most obscene corruption of God's dream. But throughout history, God has kept on calling on behalf of the creation God loves. God's call raises up prophets and raised up God's own Son on the cross. Even in these latter days of scarce vision and shrinking institutional forms of the church, God keeps on calling.

God keeps calling, and a little boy haunted by the voice calling him in the night gets up again. Eli understands. Eli knows his time is past. He knows the horrible retribution awaiting his faithless sons. But all that matters to him, this flawed mentor for Samuel, is that the Lord is calling. In the midst of his weakness and spiritual desert, Eli can yet place the hand of this boy into the hand of the God calling him to be a prophet. It must have broken Eli's heart to say this: "Go, lie down; and if he calls you, you shall say, 'Speak, Lord, for your servant is listening' " (1 Samuel 3:9).

Can you think of your congregation as Eli, still at the table and building new tables, helping the next generation hear the call? And then "the Lord came and stood there, calling as before, 'Samuel. Samuel!' And Samuel said, 'Speak, for your servant is listening" (1 Samuel 3:10).

In a church in Montgomery, Alabama, following the arrest of Rosa Parks, Martin Luther King Jr., a latter-day Samuel, faced a crowded room of Elis close to the Ark and said, "As you know, my friends, there comes a time when people get tired of being trampled over by the iron feet of oppression." The church erupted. "If we are wrong, God Almighty is wrong! If we are wrong, Jesus of Nazareth was merely a utopian dreamer and never came down to earth! If we are wrong, justice is a lie."[15]

Martin showed up in a time when the word of the Lord was rare, just as Samuel did when he answered God's call. Church, this is our time! We have been baptized and placed at the tables for a time such as this. God keeps calling, especially when there is no frequent vision. Those faithful to God stay by the Ark. And as Eli shaped Samuel, one generation shapes the next. Mission leadership is still being nurtured. God will not be without a prophet in this world.

I am struck by how much Dr. King was bogged down by his sense of how easily the word of the Lord can become rare and visions become infrequent. Like pastors, congregational leaders, or bishops, King had to walk a tight line when he was not at all certain that the voice calling him in the night was the Lord's. He had to maintain the movement's momentum while maintaining hopes of an alliance with the federal government. He, too, had to link the public tables. He had to reconcile demands of grassroots groups with larger, national agendas and advocacy. He had to mediate between more radical figures like Stokely Carmichael and conservative ones like Roy Wilkins. He had to find a balance between opposing the government on the Vietnam War and working with the government on the war on poverty. As he arrived in Memphis, he was weary and depressed. The antipoverty drive was stalled. The Vietnam War overshadowed everything. Violence was becoming part of the movement for some. His inner circle was consumed by infighting.

Do you sometimes feel that weariness in your bones? I do. I can remember my Samuel days as a reproach. Was it that long ago we were fighting the scourge of drugs and fighting for racial justice in Jackson Heights, Queens, and I received death threats? All of us wonder what has become of our visions in a time when the word of the Lord seems rare and there are no frequent visions. But King, weary and worried, went to Memphis because where any person is not free, no one is free. I can imagine him going to a mining town in West Virginia or a migrant farm in Michigan.

But in Memphis the searing vision of God's dream of justice, the flaming truth of the word of the Lord burned brightly for him again. He spoke to us and for us in our own time. He reminded us of the power of staying near the Ark, of confidence that God will call again and again and raise up prophets among our Elis.

So we come to the table now and rest by the Ark. We receive the God who keeps calling us to life and the struggle for justice through the bread and wine. And we listen to the latter-day Samuel as he continues to speak to us from Memphis on the eve of his journey from life to death to life:

> Well, I don't know what will happen now. . . . We've got some difficult days ahead. But it really doesn't matter with me now, because I've been to the mountaintop and I don't mind. Like anybody, I would like to live a long life. Longevity has its place. But I'm not concerned about that now. I just want to do God's will, and He's allowed me to go up to the mountain.
>
> And I've looked over, and I've seen the Promised Land. I may not get there with you, but I want you to know tonight, that we as a people will get to the Promised Land. So I'm happy tonight; I'm not worried about anything. I'm not fearing any man. Mine eyes have seen the glory of the coming of the Lord.[16]

Each of our communities has Elis, Samuels, Martin Luther King Jrs. We learn to love the most vulnerable at the kitchen table. We learn to have a heart for justice and equity for all people at the altar table. Mission today is building tables, expanding tables, inviting others to tables, allowing ourselves to be invited to the tables of others. The voice calling out into the night is calling you. We have been baptized for this moment.

One More Table

One Sunday a number of years ago as I ended my sermon for the first worship service, I noticed a boy about ten years old had begun to stare at me. His mother had died, and his grandmother, with the church, was providing a table for him.

At the next service, he and his grandmother attended again. He stared at me through the service, and the intensity of his gaze grew during the sermon. As I ended the sermon he was hearing for the second time, I noticed that he smiled and whispered to his grandmother. When I greeted them at the door at the end of the service, his staring continued.

"What gives with the little guy?" I asked his grandmother as he looked up at us.

"Your grandmother," she said.

My grandmother had died the previous week. In the sermon, I told of my last visit with her, of setting a table together. She was in a nursing home, and she was having trouble remembering things and people. I had not seen her in a while, and I was worried that she would not remember me. As I entered the room, I saw her hunched in a chair in the corner surrounded by shrines of her identity on TV tables. They included a large-print Bible; family pictures, including one of me in a Little League uniform; her confirmation certificate; and some other things.

This beloved woman who sang love songs to me as a child looked up, and her vacant eyes beginning to crinkle in recognition. She rose. "I think you belong to me," she said. Then "Stevie!" As she called out my name, I realized that it is a holy thing to be remembered, and to remember. I told the congregation about the table we set together: I placed bread and wine between us, and we began to remember the tables.

"Grandma, the body of Christ for you."

"Grandma, the blood of Christ for you."

As we embraced before I left, she said this: "Thank you for remembering me."

As I ended the sermon, I pointed to the altar table, inviting people to the Eucharist. "This table will be crowded. My grandmother will be here. We say it, don't we? With angels and archangels and all the company of heaven, in every time and every place."

And that is when the boy whispered to his grandmother, "Mom's here!" And he wanted to hear the sermon again, to hear about his mother being at the table with him and our risen Christ. We have a faith and a story a ten-year-old can understand if we will only recommit our lives to sharing it and living it.

In the beginning . . . all through our lives . . . in eternity . . . there is a table set for us and all creation.

Then I saw a new heaven and a new earth. . . . And I saw the holy city, the new Jerusalem, coming down out of heaven from God. . . . And I heard a loud voice from the throne saying,

> "See, the home of God is among mortals.
> [God] will dwell with them;
> they will be [God's] peoples,
> and God . . . will be with them;
> [God] will wipe every tear from their eyes.
> Death will be no more;
> mourning and crying and pain will be no more,
> for the first things will have passed away."

. . . "See, I am making all things new." (Revelation 21:1-5)

Read and Reflect, Discuss and Reflect

1. Read Luke 18:1-8 and 1 Samuel 3:1-20. What do the passages say to you, at this time and place, about God, the church, and the wider world?

2. What is your vision for how your congregation can live into Isaiah's promise "You shall be called the repairer of the breach, the restorer of streets to live in" (58:12)?

3. At times near the altar table or in your community, at your neighbors' tables, or around your kitchen table, have you sensed God's voice calling you or your congregation, like Samuel, to a particular mission?

4. Look at the diagram on page 107. Does your congregation already have companions in these arenas; that is, is there a web of interconnection, perhaps still thin and fragile, that can be strengthened and expanded? Who are these companions? Name names—both people and institutions or agencies.

5. Recall a recent story of persistence and public exposure that has moved you, that has made an impression. What does it illustrate or teach that might be applied to your congregation's mission table?

Notes

1. Martin Luther, *Luther's Small Catechism with Evangelical Worship Texts*, trans. Timothy J. Wengert (Augsburg Fortress, 2008), 21.

2. "Now Rest beneath Night's Shadow," *Evangelical Lutheran Worship* 568 (Augsburg Fortress, 2006). Text: Paul Gerhardt, 1607–1676; trans. composite.

3. Bishop Claude E. Payne and Hamilton Beazley, *Reclaiming the Great Commission* (Jossey-Bass, 2000).

4. Heidi Neumark, presentation at the 2002 Conference of Bishops, Vancouver, British Columbia.

5. Nikki Giovanni, *Those Who Ride the Night Winds* (Wm. Morrow, 1983).

6. David L. Tiede, "Evangelism Today: Lutheran Theology and Practice" (Hein-Fry Lecture Series, 2004).

7. Ernst Troeltsch, *The Social Teaching of the Christian Churches*, trans. Olive Wyon (Westminster John Knox, 1992).

8. Ronald Heifetz, Alexander Grashow, and Marty Linsky, *The Practice of Adaptive Leadership* (Harvard Business Press, 2009), xii.

9. Check out these community organizing networks for opportunities and resources available in your area.
   - DART (Direct Action and Research Training Center): www.thedartcenter.org
   - The Gamaliel Foundation: www.gamaliel.org
   - IAF (Industrial Areas Foundation): www.industrialareasfoundation.org
   - IVP (The InterValley Project): www.intervalleyproject.org
   - NPA (National Peoples Action): www.npa-us.org
   - PICO (People Improving Communities through Organizing): www.piconetwork.org

10. Evangelical Lutheran Church in America Research and Evaluation, "Report on New Congregational Ministries from 2006 to the Present," November 2012.

11. Frederick Douglass, "An Address on West India Emancipation (3 August 1857)," *Selected Speeches and Writings*, ed. Philip S. Foner and Yuval Taylor (Chicago Review Press, 2000).

12. Fred Craddock, quoted in Jeffrey Krehbiel, *Reflecting with Scripture on Community Organizing* (Acta, 2010).

13. Martin Luther King Jr., *Where Do We Go from Here: Chaos or Community?* (Beacon Press, 1968).

14. Ibid.

15. Martin Luther King Jr., "Speech to the Montgomery Improvement Association" (December 1955).

16. Martin Luther King Jr., "I've Been to the Mountaintop" (Memphis, TN, April 3, 1968).